Wicked Legends

by

Yda H. Addis

Yda H. Addis

Legends—"such was the gossip of the vulgar, which started from a foundation of truth, poetizes, and reverses things and forms, giving to them strange, indefinite or mysterious character which so delights the human imagination...."

From Yda Addis's short story *The Street of Don Juan Manuel.*

Editor: Sterling Saint James

Copyright: 2018, S. S. J. Trust

ISBN-10: 0-9893695-5-2
ISBN 13: 978-0-9893695-5-8

Parhelion House, Inc. Publisher
info@ParhelionHouse.com

Cover: *Mexico Lindo*, by Nancy Glenn-Nieto

Graphics and Introduction: Sterling Saint James

Victorian lines by Vecteezy

Introduction

Caution! Reading further may cause some individuals to have a shift in their perceptions: You are about to meet a 19th century writer who some have called clairvoyant, while others refer to her as a psychic, but before she disappeared in 1902 many thought she was crazy. Perhaps the latter could be true or was it a disguise?

The writer's name was Yda Hillis Addis, but she signed her short stories with Y. H. Addis, or Yda Addis. She was born in Lawrence, Kansas Territory in 1857, but spent half of her life in the country of Mexico. Her professional writing career began when she was twenty-three years old in 1880 with a short fictional romantic story published in the San Franciscan bi-monthly political journal *The Argonaut*.

Her debut in *The Argonaut* was so successful that for the next fifteen years hardly an issue appeared without one of her stories. It was during 1885 to 1889 when she lived in Mexico City that she wrote this collection of *Wicked Legends*.

With compact prose, murky magical realism, and fantasy, Addis guided her readers away from modern horror stories of the 19th century, into a voyage in time to centuries past where things and places were oddly similar, but not.

For example she offered her readers a view of the deep dark lush tropical jungles of la tierra caliente of Mexico; then to discover by the light of a bonfire dancing devils who leaped and contorted with a strange uncanny nature, which seemed to the reader that they were to partake of the character of a rite or service. The ringmaster of the soiree, the Sorcerer, then "turned toward his house with an awful gesture, and there came forth two black slave-like women, both stark naked, who led between them the girl, the Sorcerer's daughter." What happened to the girl? The question answered in the chapter *The Devil's Plains*.

Ghastly ghosts, human hangings, false-adultery, and murder, murder, murder! Here is a collection of psychological thrillers employing drama, dismay, and mystery, but also Addis embellishes some legends handed-down through the oral tradition from the 16th to the 18th centuries in Mexico. With literary turns, and twists she thoroughly entertains her readers.

—Sterling Saint James

Contents

The Wailing Woman

"La Llorona"
A Legend of Mexico adapted into English
By
Yda Addis
Appeared in *The Argonaut* March 10, 1888

It was three o'clock in the morning. The bells of the cathedral and the palace, far away, struck the hour, as we traversed a lonely, silent street toward the suburbs of Mexico City. We had been keeping vigil with a wounded man, a compatriot of mine, and had overstayed our watch, for he was frantic with delirium, and we feared to transfer him to the care of the inexperienced and rather careless persons who should succeed us.

We walked on briskly; for it was long hours past the

time when coaches and tram-cars were running. We were in San Cosme, and in front of the great, massive structure which the wife of ex-Marshal Bazaine has claimed from the government as an imperial gift to her traitorous husband. The facade of this building curves in such fashion as to form an offset or alcove on the street, and before we reached it I thought I saw a woman's figure stealing along in its denser shadow, and I felt a thrill of compassion for her, as one of the poor children of the night. She was not to be seen when we came near the spot, but a moment later a piercing cry rang out near us—a long drawn wail of suffering and horror.

I grasped the arm of my companion. "Some woman is in distress—we must go to her rescue. We are both armed, more than heaven!"

But he threw his arm about me, and forced me forward at a quick pace that was almost a run; and so unexpected was his behavior that I could not resist.

"Come on! Come on!" he whispered hoarsely, as I shook myself free from his clasp, "we must hurry! We must go on quickly!"

"I would not have believed you could desert a fellow creature in trouble!" I said with indignation, "and beyond all, a woman. It is not like you, Federico." Because I had seen his courage tried by venomous serpents in tierra caliente; and in encounters with highwaymen in the Sierras; and I had heard of his coolness and daring in a combat with Apaches in Northern Chihuahua.

"Hush! Hush!" he answered, panting. "You do not know what you are saying. We did not leave a mortal woman—the voice you hear is the cry of La Llorona. Look over there at the sentinel!"

We were near one of the points where a watchman stands all night in the middle of the thoroughfare, and following my companion's gestures, I saw the officer, fallen upon his knees in the circle of light cast by his lantern; the great capuchin hood of his cape was pulled over his head, and every line of his figure betokened abject fear and horror. There was something uncanny in the sight, for the policemen of Mexico are not impressionable material. And through the silent, empty street those dreadful cries still went ringing wildly, surely sufficient motive for such a display of terror. The sound seemed to float away, and down a by-street toward the equestrian statue of Charles IV, growing fainter and fainter in the distance.

"Let's go," said my companion; "yes, I am skeptic, and I sneer at spiritualism, and ghosts, and phantoms; but, nevertheless, I think there is not a man or woman in Mexico who would not tremble at the voice of Luisa La Llorona."

***

In the year 1584, Luisa Haro was known as the most beautiful girl in Mexico, and the most unpresumptuous. Her father had brought her from Spain when she was ten years old, and, he had died four years later, had left her without family, so far it was known. She was a clever needle-woman, and a maker of artificial silk flowers, and her skill found ready employment for churchly uses, notwithstanding the enormous quantity of such work done in the convents. Her little home was located in a lovely *callejuela*, or bystreet, almost like an alley, in the shadow of the cloister-walls of one of the guilds that chiefly employed her, and here she lived, forlornly enough, indeed, as is the fate of a woman who dwells quite alone; but her days were virtuous and tranquil. It did not matter to her when the gallants came stealing at nightfall into that rincón apartado—that out-of-the-way corner, and occupied the narrow passage in the dusty midnight darkness. Her shuttered widows and doors were closed and barred at sunset; and none of the delicate, scented fingers that tapped on those clumsy defenses ever sounded the "Open Sesame!" to the girl they sheltered. Luisa was the despair of all the happy, dissolute blades of the vice-regal court of New Spain. Her neighbors in the lonely alley had mixed feeling about the girl, uncertain whether to respect and commend her severe integrity or to disparage her, as one who is denied the natural passions and pleasant frailties of humanity.

But a change came about when the girl was about twenty years old. The gossips of the neighborhood began to whisper that the shutters of Luisa's window now creaked slightly open, and that her voice was heard at the crevice in converse with one who came not tentatively and doubting, but with the confident, assured step of a man who knows the welcome that awaits him. And soon it was told about, originating in one of the vague, indefinite ways in which such things do transpire, that this complacent wooer was Nuño, Marquis of Montes-Claros. So it was that Luisa assumed a new importance in the eyes of those about her, as what happens under like conditions.

One night—a night when the dashing rain scourged the black walls of the cloister, to the mournful accompaniment of the moaning owls in the belfry—one of the parish good men was hurrying home through the narrow alley where Luisa lived, when he saw before him something that made him pause and tremble. He was of the timid bourgeois class that carried no weapon, no knife, nor slender deadly rapier swung from his belt.

The night was dark, almost to palpability. No ray of light fell into the alley, except the dim ray from the little lantern, swinging before the rude image of some saint in a niche near the tablet on the wall, at the entrance of the alley where it opened with a blunt angle into a wider thoroughfare.

That ray, falling through the weather-stained pane of the lantern, was dim and fitful, and almost seemed to make the darkness denser, and more concrete than the shapes that the honest wayfarer thought he saw flitting along the wall. Now these might be some of the gallants that were always wrangling hereabouts for the sweet sake of Luisa, albeit there had been a notable falling-off in their attendance, since it was rumored she had finally hearkened to the voice of one of their number. Or—and the hair of the honest fellow bristled at the idea—it might even be Don Nuño himself, and his worship, by all accounts, would not hesitate to spit like a curlew from the marshes on one whom he might meet poaching on his woman. So, fearing to be mistaken for a gallant, the honest citizen shrunk into himself, and flattened his portliness against the convent wall as best might be. And the vague shapes passed him by in silence, unperceiving.

He repented timidity the next morning, and reviled himself for a fool and a coward, when the neighborhood thrilled to the news of the flight of Luisa Haro. Her door stood ajar, and her poor belongings were left undisturbed. All the evidence pointed to the fact that her flight was voluntary and deliberate, and the popular theory was unanimous in declaring that her comrade must be Nuño, Marquis of Montes-Claros. It was this couple, no doubt, whom the good man had seen stealing away through the darkness, and his repentance was keen that he had not followed them, to possess himself of that knowledge of their movements and destination that would have made him important among his fellows.

From that day, her old-time neighbors knew nothing of Luisa Haro, except that some one whose affairs had taken him to the suburb of San Cosme brought back the story that he had seen her there, blooming and with sumptuous accessories, in the balcony of a splendid mansion that was known to belong to Montes-Claros.

***

Six years after Luisa left from her home in the narrow alley, she sat in the luxurious home where Montes-Claros had placed her, brooding mournfully over her situation. The moonlight streamed through the open window and illuminated her despondent figure. In the face and form she was more beautiful than on the day she fled with Montes-Claros, but still was she not beautiful enough to keep the fickle fancy of the Spaniard. His attentions and his interest had gradually diminished, until the unhappy woman now had but too much reason to consider herself altogether deserted by him for whom she had given up all that is most dear to woman. She lacked no material comfort, it is true, thus far, but this was little consolation to a woman whose thwarted affection was as strong and unaltered as when her passionate heart first poured out its ardent incense before her lover.

She had not seen Montes-Claros for a fortnight, and she was resolved to know the worst without further horror of suspense and anxiety. She got up, and carried the infant in her arms to an alcove, behind whose silken curtains lay two older children sleeping. She laid the little one beside its brothers. She put on a long, dark, clinging cloak, left the house, and made her way to the central streets of the city.

She knew the family mansion of Montes-Claros, and shortly found herself before it. The windows of the facade were ablaze with light, and she saw that the rooms were full of a festive crowd. Nuño was there in the midst of his guests with his proud, affected mother, and beside them a young girl, tall and handsome, wearing a bridal gown.

The Luisa's heart sank like lead. She pulled the sleeve a bystander, gazing like herself through the window. "Do you know, friend, who is the young lady beside the Señor Marquis?"

"Who should it be," laughed the man she questioned, "but his novia—the bride he married this morning at ten o'clock in the chapel of the Sagrario?"

Luisa could not speak, but neither did she cry out, only stepped back from the window, and pushed her way to the open street through the eager crowd of on-lookers.

Slowly, mechanically she found her way, never rushing,

never pausing, till she reached the house in San Cosme, and let herself in at its great arched entrance, and into her own bedroom. An antique coffer stood there, an ancient cedar chest with Moresque decoration, brought from Spain by the family of Montes-Claros. In it Nuño kept, while he yet frequented the home, such odds and ends that he didn't need immediately at the time, or things at the moment that he found cumbrous.

Still under the spell of that awful, deadly quiet, Luisa opened the old chest, and took from it a dagger, a curious jeweled weapon, that Nuño had tossed in it long months since, and forgotten, though its memory had lived in the fevered brain of the woman.

Still lit only by the pallid, ghastly moonbeams, she went to the alcove where her little ones lay sleeping, and drew aside the curtains.

"Your father has forsaken us, my darling ones, and your mother wants to protect you from the miseries that await you. To God I recommend your innocent spirits."

Then, one by one, slowly, surely, fatally, she thrust the dagger into the bosom of each tender little body.

Only when the blood welled darkly up, staining the white night clothes, did the wretched mother seem to realize her dreadful doing. She gazed a moment at the heart-rending vision, and then ran forth into the streets, uttering those frightful wails that for three hundred years have continued to echo in the streets of Mexico City at varying hours and seasons—when the soul in penance can no longer endure its torture, so the devout say.

As the wailing woman ran that night, her cries aroused the city, and she was captured and recognized, when the dagger she still clutched, and her blood-stained clothes, told the tragic story, and gave the clue to discovery of her victims. There was no penalty for man's inhumanity to woman in Mexico of those days, any more than in the present; and the poor distracted instrument of crime paid the temporal penalty in this case, while the actual murderer, in fact, rather gained popularity.

During her imprisonment and trial, Luisa maintained a helpless, hopeless silence. She failed and faded day by day, and when, at last, arrived the hour of execution, she was unable to walk up the steps of the scaffold, and, not from fright, but sheer weakness, she became senseless in the arms of her bearers. The execution proceeded, but the decree of the law was done on a corpse because the noose never touched her, Luisa Haro was lifeless.

And, however justice had miscarried in the hands of human authority, the retribution of heaven proved direct and active. For, on that very May day when the woman who had trusted him went to the doom of a felon, Nuño Marquis de

Montes-Claros, was buried, having died before his honeymoon was over.

And now, centuries after, it is told that, whenever appears the Wailing Woman, the following morning sees the flowers on the tomb of Montes-Claros withered, seared, and the earth upon it dank and putrid, as if it were drenched and soaked with blood.

Y. H. ADDIS.   CITY OF MEXICO, March, 1888.

A Brace of Legends

Adapted from the Spanish of Manuel Payno.
By
Yda Addis
Appeared in *The Argonaut* January 22, 1887

The mining camp of *Plateros* is situated in the district of Fresnillo, in the State of Zacatecas, about a league distant from the town of Fresnillo. Its discovery, as related in tradition was as follows: Some silversmiths (*plateros*) were journeying toward Durango, carrying in a chest an image of Christ upon the cross, when they were overtaken by a heavy rain, and were obliged to pass the night upon one of the small hills near Fresnillo. The storm ceased, and the men, after disposing their sacred burden safely in the midst of their baggage, built a huge campfire, and, seated in a circle it supped upon their thick cakes of corn-flour and savory strips of jerked beef. It is to be supposed that, being friends all on the road, and with stomachs full, they would give free play to their tongues. In good truth, they discoursed of storms and tempests, of swollen rivers, of highway robbers, and all the dangers that menace those who travel. Then the talk turned upon themes of arithmetic and finance, and very naturally it resulted that the good fellows took stock of their exchequer, which proved to contain a joint capital of barely twenty dollars.

"If only the Lord would bestow upon us money," one of them exclaimed, in a tone of melancholy.

"Nothing is impossible to Him," replied another.

"I know that well enough; still, I don't see how we are to become rich."

"Oh, thou art a doubting Thomas. Everything comes easy to God. `If to give thee God doth will, riches shall result from swill.'"

"But it must be asked for."

"Then let us ask now."

The silversmiths accordingly kneeled before the chest that contained the holy image, and fervently recited a creed. Then, enwrapping themselves in their zarapes, they laid themselves down beside the fire, and doubtless slept. The next morning the wind had swept away the ashes where their campfire had blazed, and there, glistening in the first rays of the rising sun, was a bright and shining ingot of silver that the fire had smelted from the rock. The silversmiths, it may be readily be believed, went no further with their image, but began straightway to work the mines, where they shortly erected a chapel to Our Lady of the Silversmiths, whence the mines are named.

I do not hold myself responsible for the truth of this narrative. I can only vouch for the fact that the mines and the chapel are in existence to day. One afternoon a friend invited me to visit that same mine, and we set out accordingly. Nothing could be sadder or lonelier than the situation; a dry gulch, with a few gray houses of adobe scattered at the foot of the low hills, and a horizon line of brown hills, bare of verdure—such is Plateros. It is, however, very rich, the leads of dense sulfates cropping out on the surface. As my knowledge of mining is of the slightest, I suggested to my companion that we should visit the church, whose architecture is fine, and its dimensions all too ample for the few of the faithful in the little town.

"Before we go into the church," remarked my companion, "I wish to relate to you a tradition."

"You have the word," I answered," and that with all my heart. As the botanist go nosing about in search of unknown plants, and the mineralogists after veins of ore, so I shall get out of hearing mass by listening to a tradition."

"Once upon a time, then," my friend began, "a poor man came up the road, driving a small, lean donkey. This animal carried a little chest of pinchbeck rings, ear-rings, looking-glasses, and the like rubbish for sale among the rancheros. In short, this was a peddler. When he had arrived at a cliff in one of the hills, he unloaded the donkey and turned it loose to grass at will, while he sat down upon his pack-saddle. After a time another wayfarer appeared and came to sit down by the former. They talked a while, smoked their cigarettes, and then lay down peacefully to sleep, for these were brothers, traveling together, and partners in business. He who had driven the donkey fell asleep very shortly, but Francisco, the other, began to think that if he were master of his brother's money and goods he would have enough to support him, and would be subject to the command of none. This flame kindled in his mind was fanned by Satan, and he determined to carry out the idea. He observed his brother's respiration, and on tiptoe, with his lips apart and his eyes wide and rolling, he lifted up a great, black stone, and holding it above his brother's head, let it fall. A dull crash told that the sleeper's head was crushed to atoms. After a moment a stream of blood crept from beneath the stone. No sooner did the murderer see that red current run, bathing the rocks, than, like another Cain, he began to rush frenzied from place to place, tearing his locks, and beating his head against the boulders. Finally, desperate, he turned to the chapel of Our Lady of the Silversmiths, and there he wept a very torrent of tears, calling on his Maker to show him mercy. [You see, the poor devil, not withstanding the course of justice was not very prompt then on Mexican soil, feared to find himself uncomfortably well fitted by a halter.] Well, he wept and cried, striking his sinful head against the steps of the altar, and called upon the Lord to pardon and save him, accursed criminal as he was. In the midst of his lamentations he felt a soft touch upon the shoulder, and turning his head:

"`Oh, my brother!' he cried; `have pity! If thou art a shade, if thou hast come hither from another world, have pity and forgive me!'

"`What kind of a trick do you call that,' demanded the other, `to go away and leave the beast and load unwatched and me alone and sleeping?'

"`My brother, I have killed thee!'

"`Killed me! but I'm alive!' replied the murdered man, mechanically inspecting himself closely.

"`None the less, I hurled a great stone upon your head, and saw your blood gush forth and your brains spattered around.'

"The other passed his hands over his head, and, while he found no wound, he experienced a slight pain beneath the touch. `But, my brother, explain this thing.'

"`Oh! I am a sinner, vile and accursed! But the Lord has seen my repentance, and He has restored thee to life. Let us pray.' "

"The two brothers fell upon their knees, and prayed long and devoutly. Going later to the scene of the murder, they found there the stone still covered with fresh blood."

When his recital had reached this point, my friend said, seeing me open my eyes wide, "Come in, and you may see the stone." And on going in, in fact, I saw and touched, in one corner of the chapel, a great black bolder capable of demolishing not merely the head of a man, but of an elephant.

I hold myself responsible for the account of this miracle no more than of the other. It is a tradition which I relate to the reader as it was told to me.

Y. H. ADDIS.   MEXICO, January 9, 1887.

La Pila del Corazón

The Curious Legend of
"The Fountain of the Sacred Heart."
By
Yda Addis
Appeared in *The Argonaut* June 18, 1887

J am a nervous person, in the sense of being bothered by noise—irritable, perhaps, would rather be the word—and a boisterous child caused me to move from the place I called home. I relinquished my once quiet room on the inner court, where my belongings were so accustomed all that they seemed to fall into their places mechanically, at the slightest touch of the hand. But he who works with his brain must care for his tool.

I moved to the Hotel Alexander, across the city almost from my former residence that was located on the street of El Sagrado Corazón de Jesús—the Sacred Heart of Jesus. Many of the streets in Mexico City are named like that—for some old church or convent which formerly stood in the street—aye, which still stands, though now converted to state or secular use. The Church of El Sagrado Corazón has not been so converted. Its parish was a very wealthy one, and it saved the church, by buying in, from confiscation. This temple is today the richest in the city, and the only one with the right to ring its bells for longer than three minutes at a time. But the gardens that used to skirt the sacred edifice have long been parceled out into city lots, now built over with many houses, and the convent buildings are divided off, and used as private homes, as shops, as apartment houses, or what you will, except for only their old time churchly uses.

For long after the Reform Laws went into operation, the Church of El Sagrado Corazón de Jesús faced on to a little place or square in which a fountain flowed. This square was once the main interior court of the church possessions, and it was only some five years ago that an investigative spirit discovered that the bit of ground still rested under the church's title. Fired with indignant zeal, he reported the matter to the authorities, the little plaza was pounced upon, and sold to the enterprising individual in question, who at once proceeded to build thereupon this large Hotel Alexander, in which, owing to the good fortune of its owner in finding a central site not closed around by other buildings, "all the back rooms are front rooms," as an admiring American journalist put the phrase.

As I have said, the hotel is bounded by the streets of El Sagrado Corazón—La Calle del Sagrado Corazón goes past the front; on the right, and between the hotel and the church, the Estampa del Sagrado Corazón; in the rear, Callejón del Sagrado Corazón; and on the left, the plaza of the same name, in which the fountain stands, it having been situated at one side of the original square, so that it now stands in a sort of open, alcove-like court, an offset from the side street which joins it to the main thoroughfare in front. This Pila or fountain supplies water for domestic use to a large section of the city hereabouts, and at certain hours of the day the *aguadores* come to fill their picturesque, three-handled *chochocoles*. Wearing their leather harnesses, studded and clamped with brass, their heads covered with straw caps sewed with leather, the quaint earthen vessels strapped from their foreheads by broad leather bands, in the stolid wooden faces, and rapid, machine-like movements, the *aguadores* appear almost like machines; and yet there is probably no other type in the city nearly so picturesque as theirs. It is a favorite resource with me to watch them daily, as they gather around the circular wall of the fountain, dipping up the water while they gossip. The *aguador*, reticent as he is with the rest of the world, is genial and communicative with his own class. I have no doubt they criticize most freely the slender shanks of young Ponce de Leon, at whose hands their chief has just pocketed a good sized tip for the transmission of a letter to Blanca de Nieves. For of this fraternity are the Mercury's of surreptitious or clandestine love-making, thanks to the *aguador's* faculty of easy contact with the fair ladies, who may find difficulties, no less than the mistresses they serve, in coming forth to a position accessible to letters.

Accustomed, then, to this daily marshalling of the clan about the Pila beneath my window, their absence was the first thing that struck me, as I threw the curtains open one morning when I had arrived on the early train from a trip into Morelos. Nor did the water-carriers make their appearance, as usual, some hours later, at the time when they supply the kitchens with water for preparation of the noon day breakfast. It was not for lack of water in the Pila—it was overflowing its brink.

"What has become of all the *aguadores*?" I asked the man who performs the offices of housemaid for our corridor.

Ciriaco shrugged his shoulders. "*Quien sabe*, señorita; it is the day they do not come." Nor could all my insistence elicit further information.

They were back again the following day, however, much to my relief, for I had feared the walk-out might be permanent. And the next morning, taking up my *Diario*, which is usually the most prompt of the daily journals to chronicle current news, I chanced to note among its *gacetilla* a paragraph, of which the translation runs as follows:

"The day before yesterday marked the date on which, once every month, the water in the Pila del Sagrado Corazón de Jesús becomes undrinkable for twenty-four hours, whether filtered or not. What can be the cause of this peculiar periodical manifestation?"

The languid tone of curiosity made me smile. I could but compare this with the energy of American journalism, realizing how, in the event of such a phenomenon among ourselves, the ground would have been thronged with rival reporters of the local and general press; how they would have camped upon the spot, tasting the water every third second, and causing it to be analyzed almost as often, and tracing the stream back to its fountain-head, rather than that the mystery should escape them. I set inquiry on foot, myself, in an access of the reportorial instinct, realizing the importance of the efforts all the while; I am free to confess my discernment was admirable sustained, the officials to whom I applied manifesting only a lukewarm interest, palpably prompted by a sense of gallantry, or else the more honest phase of avowed indifference.

"It has been so for many years," those of the latter contingent would aver; "the effect is the same, whatever may be the cause. It is only one day in a month, and that can be endured. Indeed, it is even the better for the *aguadores*, since the farther they carry the water, the larger will be their fee."

Vexed and disillusioned by this want of interest in the official powers, I directed myself next to the *aguadores*. Distrust of my race and my sex made the fraternity even more than usually non-committal. Then applying my favorite theory of the unfailing victory of the cultivated mind over the untrained, I told the maestros—for they will suffer themselves to be addressed only thus as "Master"—that it was my firm conviction the taint in the fountain resulted from its uncleanly condition. At this, the group I addressed, unlimbered their tongues no little, volubly assuring me that the reservoir was cleaned out every week; and in effect, some three days later, I saw a little army of them invade the plaza, plug up the channel with a bit of wood, and then, climbing into the great tub-like basin, scrub it out briskly and completely with brushes of *zacaton*-root. This process was repeated twice during the month.

Strangely enough, neither the fact of the water's periodical unsavory disposition, nor the obstacles I encountered in seeking an explanation of the occurrence, inspired in me repulsion or distaste for the fountain itself. On the contrary, I grew really fond of the rough, inartistic stone structure, set like an enormous muffin-ring at the side of the bare and treeless plaza. Especially at night did it seem less harsh and unattractive; there were hushed the strident voices of the parrots that all day long squawked on their respective perches, one at each of the three little pottery shops behind the hotel; then no longer could I hear the un-tuned piano hammered all day long across the way. The grim, dingy facades of the houses around the narrow plaza were softened in the darkness, and an old-fashioned lantern, swung from a wire extended from one of my balconies to another opposite, cast a light that wavered and shifted with a certain romantic quality, as the lamp swayed in the wind. It gave a sense of companionship in the lonely nights when I was wakeful, to listen to the plash of the water, pouring into the basin below, and often I would arise and sit in the balcony, that I might hear it more plainly. I had been extremely busy for some days, and had lost the run of time, when I awakened one night, softly, without a start, and with a curious, impersonal sense of interest in something—I knew not what. I arose and wrapped myself warmly, and went into the balcony of my little sitting-room, giving on the back street at right angles to the side toward the plaza, and overlooking, would one but lean over the balustrade, the entrance to the church of El Sagrado Corazón. Leaning and looking, still with that indefinite and tranquil expectation, I saw two figures emerge form the gateway of the temple, and move along the street toward me. I smiled. "Some young woman with an over-complaisant *dueña* has come to keep a tryst at the church, and has found the lover recreant." I concluded this because there was somewhat of despondency and heaviness in their movement. Then it occurred to me that they might have come to invoke the offices of the church in behalf of the sick or dying. They came nearer, and passed beneath my window, and then I saw that instead of the matronly protector, the taller shape was the figure of a priest in his long cassock.

What happened next became the strangest chapter of my life. I could swear on my death-bed that no sound broke the calm silence of the night, save the falling of the water in the fountain, and the insistent warbles of a mocking-bird near by, that would sing all night long when there was moonlight, its voice sounding weird and unnatural at such unwonted hours. Yet, notwithstanding, I know—I know—that I heard every word spoken by that strange pair as if their thoughts had echoed in my brain. It was as if I were the vehicle for the formulating of the unuttered thought of incorporate brains—as if some subtle medium of communication conveyed to me what they said.

"I beg, no I implore you, Beatriz," the man's volition sounded in my brain, "my life-long peace, my life itself, is in your hands."

The girl stopped short, and wheeled about, throwing out her hands with a gesture of disdain. "Andres Molina! Are you mad?" I felt her reply. "Was it for this you opened the door of my room? I thought I had found a friend in you—the confessor of my mother; I thought you condemned this worldly, wicked scheme of hers to wed me to old Díaz, and that you had brought me here to take counsel as to how we should persuade her to change her mind. Instead, you use this clandestine meeting to tell me that you love me. You! A priest! A friar! Holy Mary! How evil a thing must I be that I can inspire so base a passion?"

"But listen, Beatriz. I have loved you so long—even in your childhood, before I took the vows, I loved you ever. That makes a difference. It is not as if this had begun beneath the frock of the priest. You do not love me? You must! You shall! For what other purpose did I counsel your mother to bring you here to the care of the good sisters? I had no way to speak with you at home—you chose another confessor—you always were self-willed! Ah, sweet! From now on I shall confess you—and of most tender sins. We will flee—to an island—to a desert—us alone where there in some solitude."

He threw his arms around her with a quick, impassioned movement. But the girl freed herself with a sudden wrench, stepping backward. They had come close to the fountain; I could see her hand gleam white, as she leaned upon it on the dark stone rim, and the glitter of a great diamond upon her finger. The long dark cloak she wore fell to her feet, and I could see her clearly in the brilliant moonlight—a creature of passing beauty, garbed in the Manola costume of Andalusia. "She has come form some masked ball," I said to myself; "they have taken her from the dance to seclude her in the convent." Even at the distance I was, and but by moonlight, I could tell the look of scorn and repulsion on her face, as she looked at the priest.

"Dastard! False friend!" she stung; "dishonored priest. This is indeed too much. My mother shall know the teachings that you offer!"

Standing over against her, the priest's handsome, dark browed countenance underwent a change—the change from one fierce passion to another.

"You threaten me, little fool? Betray me to your mother! But that dear mother is beata—a devotee. Already your little piety has terrified and estranged her. She sees you as a brand amid the burning. If I should tell her tomorrow the devil carried you bodily away for your sins she would not question. She has a convenient faith in miracles, you see!"

"What then? Indeed, I know her weakness all too well. I have a stronger stay. Am I a child—a poor, weak creature like the women here—your Mexican creoles, who submit to whatever yoke is laid upon them?   Remember that I am a Spanish woman—we Andaluces have wills of our own. Bah! I let myself be brought to the convent, to gain time.   Have you forgotten that there is an old law by which lovers may appeal from the restraints imposed by arbitrary parents, to the aid of justice, which reunites them, if no unlawful obstacle exists? While I have been here in sanctuary, where I had hopped to gain your influence to mollify my mother, my lover has invoked this law in our behalf."

"Your—lover? Accepted—lover?"

The girl smiled with some malice. "Even so, you did not know? Why then, it would appear that my good mother, for all her blind devotion, lacked somewhat of confidence toward her dear confessor. My lover? Yes! So true, so noble, so deeply loved, that other men beside seem all like ghosts. Here was cause enough that I should despise your suit, even though it involved not the monstrous thought of sacrilege. You dare to turn your eyes where León worships?"

Then, even as I heard through the silence the sense of their unspoken word, I saw through the darkness, as before, the movements that befell. I saw the priest strike down the girl with a brutal, coward blow, and then stand like a man dazed by the sight of what he had done. I saw him flee away to the inner regions of the convent, casting behind him guilty, frightened glances, and presently return, bearing where with to conceal the evidences of his sin. I saw him pry up and lift aside the great stone flags in the centre of the fountain, and lay the dead girl in the hollow he formed beneath them, laying the basalt slabs again in place. I even noted the murky state of the water. Then he slipped away into the shadows of the church, and the fountain plashed as ever, and the mocking-bird sang on.

***

Early the following day I received a call. My visitor was a priest—a Cuban Spaniard, whom I had long known as the Cura of Pachuca. He was a short, plump, rosy, pleasant man, with the softest hands, the gentlest voice, and the kindliest eyes imaginable. A true churchman, too was he; that is to say, a thorough man of the world, using tactfully all knowledge and experience to the glory of his faith and its proliferation, yet never obtruding his religious beliefs and missions; merry, philosophical, with tastes inclined toward literature and art—such was the Cura Santa Lucía. I welcomed no guest more gladly, and his company was particularly grateful this day, when I was in a state of mind half dreaminess, half exaltation, from the experience of the night.

"I am going to be your neighbor," said the good priest, presently, when we had chatted awhile of indifferent things; "Yes, I have been appointed to the curacy of El Sagrado

Corazón."

I was very sincerely pleased—from selfish reasons—for I was glad to be able to see more of the Cura. Glad from more altruistic motives, knowing what a difficulty it must have been for this clever, scholarly man with his fine social gifts, had been a stay in the mountains, surrounded by rude and brawling miners.

"Truthfully, I did not like it out there. It did not make me happy. Yet, take it how you will, it is a good world this. I know none better."

Favorite stock phrases of the Cura, such were the words he now spoke in answer to my observations regarding the change. From this, nothing was easier than to pass to the subject of the church of his duties, its rich, aristocratic congregation, and the special privileges enjoyed by the guild. Many of these advantages, the Cura went on to say, had accrued to that particular benefice through the energy and holiness of a priest whose duty as chaplain of the convent, and in various other positions of dignity and trust, had been at the middle of the seventeenth century. The zeal and ability of this cleric—for he had risen to high ecclesiastic rank—had been themes for many glorifying records in the archives of the church.

"I have just been reading up in them," the Cura said, "for surely it becomes me to know the history of my living.

Among the rest is a very curious story of a miracle," he went on, with an odd twinkle in his bright eyes, "a miracle performed by this holy and austere brother, Friar Andres Molina."

I started at the name.

"There was a widow in Mexico then," the priest went on, "a Spaniard—an Andalusian with one child. This daughter, Beatriz, was a brilliant girl, with independent notions of her own that interfered with the mother's proposition. Therefore, La Manola, as she was called from always wearing the Andalusian garb, was promised in marriage to an elderly man named Díaz, and resisting the match, she was imprisoned here in the convent of this church, where Friar Andres Molina prayed with and for her, until, pronouncing her an accursed thing, and invoking the devil to come and take his own, her cell was thrown open—and found to be empty."

The good Father concluded his recital with an indulgent smile, then: "We of the clergy are not less than human," he said, "and Friar Andres Molina doubtless was in innocent collusion with one of the lovers of Doña Beatriz; for she appears to have had suitors galore. Indeed, the record farther states, as an evidence of her wicked power over men, that one León Aviles killed himself at the gates of the convent, as soon as the fact of her disappearance was verified."

"León! It was for the jealousy of him that she was

slain!" I said. And the Cura looked at me as if doubting my sanity. Then, because I knew the liberal mind of the man, and his tolerance of theories that many would deem heretical, I told him the story of my visions of the night. He seemed not incredulous, not greatly surprised.

"These are mysterious phrases in this life of ours," he said, "and strange, inscrutable happenings. Moreover, in those half barbarous days, the men of the cassock too often abused their power. What is the day of the month that the water becomes undrinkable in the fountain?"

I started to my feet. "I had forgotten, having slept late when once I fell asleep. But—I think it must be today."

And in soon the tank was overflowing its brim, and no busy movements went on in the little square.

"For the curiosity of it, I will look up the record," said the priest, "and see if this phenomenon coincides with the miraculous disappearance of Beatriz. And if it be possible, an examination shall be made beneath the fountain."

I know not what pretext the good priest made, nor what pressure he brought to bear. Only there is one of the ministers, whose Semitic countenance bespeaks all the subtleties of diplomacy, who is deeper in fellowship with the clergy than he would care to have the Liberal party know, and it is more than likely his influence was invoked. I only know the Cura knocked at my door at an advanced hour of the night.

"Do you care to come? Shall we call up some of your American friends to accompany you?" he said. "The dates—you understand me—coincide. I am interested beyond belief. Moreover, if that is true that we suspect, those poor relics of humanity should have Christian burial. The neighbors are asleep, and the watchmen have their instructions. Will you come?"

We woke from their chamber-door staunch, practical John Cavanaugh, and a slim young attaché of the diplomatic corps, and, wrapped in waterproofs, for a cold, small rain was misting down, we made our way through the courtyard and the shadowy great zaguán, Señor del Río, the administrator, himself giving us egress, that we might not arouse the hall porter, to wonder at and perhaps to spy on our movements. The men chosen for the work were on the ground, and the plashing stream of the Pila stilled, and its basin drained of the water. Even the cement between the lozas was already picked out, and all awaited the arrival of the Cura. The watchman from the corner had drawn near, and curiously watched the scene. The Cura gave the word; the crowbars were inserted, slowly the levers worked, and the great slabs were upraised and lifted aside. The workmen—people of the Cura, he had brought with him to the country—caught their breath at what they half saw in the dim light, with a cry of fear.   But religious feeling and respect for their priest triumphed over the natural impulse of horror and superstition, and they quietly stepped aside, removed their broad brimmed hats, and held the lanterns nearer.   Clear in the yellow light, we saw there plainly, resting in a hollow of the damp and noisome earth, as in a cradle, the form of a woman, young, and of surpassing beauty.   Her rich raiment was unstained, and her face and delicate hands looked as if she had been laid there a moment since, and not two centuries ago.   It was the hapless girl whose lovely face and Manola garb I had plainly seen through the darkness of the night, and whose sweet brave words, all unspoken, I had heard.   The Cura stooped, and lifted a silken cover from a chest of ancient Spanish cedar, marvelously carved.

"We will lay her in here."

With one accord, he and the Americans bent to take up the beauteous figure that no menial hands should profane. But at their touch, it crumbled away swiftly as fades a dream, and there lay but a handful of moldy dust, with a great sparkling diamond glittering in the midst.

Y. H. ADDIS.   CITY OF MEXICO, June, 1887.

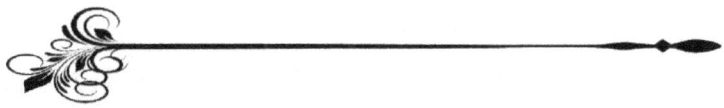

Street of the Burnt Woman

A Legend of Mexico.
By
Yda H. Addis
Appeared in *The Argonaut*, April 30, 1887

A well-known street in Mexico City is La Calle de la Quemada, or "the Street of the Burnt Woman." Named so after a romantic story, one that was written on ancient parchment papers, dusty and long forgotten, but discovered during the excavation of the catacombs of the ancient Cathedral that faces the Zócalo.

Although the lovers in this tale lived and breathed, and had their lives two centuries ago, their story, nevertheless, comes to us now full of a fresh and a vivid memory, as if it were of people we might know. And strangely enough it is a pleasant story, too, notwithstanding its dark stain of human suffering; perhaps because, tragic as were the events, the outcome of intense passions, they partook not of the taint of intrigue, of treachery and dishonor that too often characterized the love affairs of the hot-blooded Spaniards. For this is a story of love and heroic sacrifice, and the lessons it teaches are all sweet and wholesome.

Marina Anaya was one of the loveliest young ladies of Nueva Hispana. Hers was that rare beauty, at once glowing and gentle, that fills the hearts of men and women alike with tenderness. "On her sweet face a blessing!" said an old beggar woman, one day while on the on the Paseo, who turned to look at the girl. "The day seems brighter, the world seems better, since she walked by me."

In short, Marina was one of the few beings gifted with the faculty of winning the love of all. She had not an enemy in the world. She lived a simple life in her parents' home, making their lives bright, going about her daily routine with cheerfulness, and gladly taking her share of such amusement and social sunshine as was possible with the women of her era. She was no saint, Marina, but neither was she a coquette, a nag, a hypocrite, nor an empty-headed doll—but a sweet, true, pure-minded woman. It was deemed strange, in her wide circle of acquaintances, that Marina had no lover. Suitors she had many from whom all she needed was to choose. But she elected not to do so. "Why should I wed?"

She would answer when questioned; "Simply to have a husband? But what is a husband worth if I do not love him? Better that I should live "to robe the saints," as is the old adage, than to marry because it is the custom, and afterward meet a man whom I give my heart; Ay Dios! What misery. No! No! I think my parents love me; and, until they send me from their home, I will not marry, unless I fall in love." During those times, to follow one's decisions required even more than today of firmness, resolution, and singleness of purpose.

Marina had her reward. There came a replacement in the Vice-Royalty—the Viceroys were changed sometimes; the Regal Master occasionally came to the belief that his representative put the King's subjects first; for that reason, now and again, one embarked for another kingdom, to render there account of his earthly statesmanship. Thus, a new Viceroy came to Mexico, and with him came Lionel de la Montaña, a handsome young man of an old well known family, who was chosen and specially ordered by Philip the Second for the journey to the new world. He was noble, handsome, and rich. Was else could a young lady want? Among the self-indulgent youth of the day might one look for a saint? Such, indeed, was not Lionel de la Montaña; he was a soldier, who had fought well and to his own fame in the campaigns of Flanders, and he had a solder's shortcomings. But he was also brave and noble whose sins were never base nor loathsome, and, judged by the standard of the time, he was exceptionally moral and honorable.

He met Marina soon after his arrival, who shall say how and where? On the Paseo, at church, or perhaps at one of the infrequent social parties of the time? And from the first time he saw her, he lived and breathed but for Marina Anaya. He made his court with such eager assiduity that they were soon betrothed. And Marina found in him her ideal lover, the realization of that standard lacking which she had been content to live unwedded. Her every wish and aspiration were satisfied by the excellences of Lionel. If only she could convince him that it was true! For the one thing that marred her perfect happiness, the one blemish in a character otherwise all symmetrical, was the terrible strain of jealousy in his nature. It may have been the modesty of the true lover, making him feel a sense of his own unworthiness. But, whatever the motive, it seemed to him impossible that he should keep the love of Marina, widely beloved and charming as she was. When he looked at her, he could not believe that she was not a fickle, armed with the wondrous power her beauty gave her, and it maddened him to think that she might go with another.

An immediate marriage might have satisfied him of the good faith of Marina, but just after the betrothal, the death of a distant relative threw the Anayas into mourning after the fashion of the rigorous etiquette of the Spaniards, and as soon as they stopped wearing black, Lent was at hand, and no one who lays claim to good taste marries during Lenten, even now, when more liberal ideas prevailed. How much less readily then, when the entire world was under priestly rule, Lent over, Marina's father especially requested that the nuptials should be deferred until the arrival from Spain of a favorite brother, uncle of the prospective bride.

All these delays were odious and even maddening to Lionel. He tormented himself with constant brooding upon them, until the reasons of postponing the marriage seemed to him strained, frivolous, and improbable. From such a conclusion, it did not take much effort to advance a step farther, and Lionel persuaded himself that Marina was tired of him, that she had never loved him, that she desired to break the bonds of their betrothal, and that all these procrastinations were ominous tokens signifying that wish and a means of gradual approach to such a rupture. His jealous passion increased, battening upon his misery, until the man had almost become insane. And the full measure of his own suffering he held to the troubled lips of poor Marina. Every absurd pretext was to him a theme of complaint and reproach. He found a source of grievance in the situation of the Anaya dwelling, located on one of the main thoroughfares, a favorite promenade of the young Spaniards, who naturally passed by, perhaps for a glimpse of Marina's beauty. The praises lavished upon her annoyed him as much as if the girl had courted them. It had come to pass that every time they saw each other resolved itself into bitterness and reproaches, and Marina was half wild with distress. She loved Lionel most dearly, and she could not doubt the ardor of his love for her, as its very intensity was the source of his mad jealousy over the fatal charm of her beauty.

At last, one morning, Lionel passed by the house and found it closed. His morbid fancy at once pictured a rival lover behind the massive shutters of the iron-barred windows, making his suit to Marina, perhaps—winning his cause, and persuading her to discard the jealous lover. Troubled by the thought, he was quickly knocked on at the zaguán (the great street door), when a small wicket in one of the windows was opened, and a white hand—and a hand he knew, Marina's hand—was put forth, and slightly beckoned. He approached, and begged to know the lady's will. For all answer a white folded letter was held toward him. He took the missive, the window quickly closed, and he could but move away to where he could read at ease:

"My worshiped Lionel," the letter ran, "my love for you has amounted fairly to worship, since we who love first only at a mature age concentrate our affections, unfiltered away by earlier, slighter loves--I have tried then, by every tenderness, to convince you that you alone, are the only man of my heart; but I have found you insensible to these assurances. As my blind and simple affection can not inspire in you that faith which is essential to wedded happiness, and as my beauty— which I therefore hold accursed—is the terrible barrier to our perfect understanding, I have resolved, not in anger nor revenge, but in sacrifice to your love, to convert that ill-starred, fatal beauty into a living horror, that you will no longer see in it temptation to disloyalty towards you. Nothing else can cure my anxiety and distress, and I do not falter. If you love me, then you shall trust me; you will pardon my unsightliness, and we shall once more be happy. If your love shall revolt and perish for the horror I become, losing that tormenting love, you wilt find peace again. I will return to you at least the tranquility I have destroyed, either by dispelling the illusion, or by protecting your passion beneath the wings of faith. Your, MARINA."

Lionel's heart sank like lead within him, with the weight of a great misgiving. What would Marina do? To what dread deed had his madness driven her? He saw now, as if from beneath a lifted veil, the folly and the cruelty of his exactions and suspicions, and he realized the depth of the divine affection he had wronged. Full of contrition, of eagerness, of awful dread, he hastened back to the house, and abbreviating as he could the ceremonious parley at the door, he sought

Marina's father, and hurriedly told to him his fears. The two men moved through the house quietly, not to attract the attention of the gossiping servants. Marina's mother was away visiting a sick friend, and the house was still. In the ante-sala, or ante-room of the great parlor, they were overtaken by a servant.

"Don Pabilito," she exclaimed, "I came to tell you that I was here dusting a moment ago, and I found the brazier was gone. I wanted to tell someone, but Doña Claudia is away, and the Niña Marina is in her room and does not answer. ¿Quien sabe? How the thief could have come in! The porter at the door must have been asleep, sir!"

Anaya checked the girl's prattle, and sent her away. In those days, and until the last few years, it was the custom to keep in all well-appointed houses a small fie of charcoal burning in a great silver brazier in the ante-sala, for the convenience of lighting cigars or cigarettes. This brazier was indeed missing here. And through the interstices of the doors a subtle odor began to creep, tainting the air of the tightly-closed house—a strange and sickening smell, whose suggestion caused the flesh to thrill with horror, and the hair to stand erect. The two men gazed at each other an instant in shocked dismay and horror, then Don Pablo quickly led the way to Marina's bedroom, and threw open the door. A rush of noxious vapor came into Lionel's face from the room that held his love, and his first glimpse of its interior, showed him Marina, bent over the big brazier on her light-stand, with her face laid close upon its glowing coals. As her father and Lionel entered the room, she lifted herself erect, every line of her figure expressing mingled agony and the fortitude of resolution, and staggering blindly forward, she fell senseless beside her bed.

***

It was a year later that the devout gathered at the early morning mass in the Cathedral watched with interest the entrance of a wedding party, in which the groom was Lionel de la Montaña, and the bride a lady whose figure was of exquisite elegance and grace, but whose face was beyond criticism, in that it was closely covered by a black silk mask, which was not removed throughout the ceremony. From her terrible self-immolation Marina had brought her beautiful eyes unscathed in vision or appearance; and her sweet fresh lips were as perfect as of yore. But all the rest of her countenance was one frightful *cicatrice*—a thing of seams and scars and dreadful discoloration, to look on which drew shudders of horror from her nearest and dearest. But for Lionel de la Montaña her charm was omnipotent—greater now than when she was in the full flush of her soft, brilliant beauty. Amid the gross extravagance and infidelity of the Spaniard in Mexico, his loyalty and devotion to his wife never wavered, and the harmony of their perfect love and trust was never marred, till their lives, but not their hearts were sundered by the power of death, when both were far advanced in age. And the street where Marina so painfully proved her love has ever since been called "The Street of the Burnt Woman."

Y. H. Addis.   April, 1887.

The Street of the Dead Man

A Legend of Ancient Mexico
By
Yda H. Addis
Appeared in *The Argonaut* August 20, 1887

El callejón Alzures in the City of Mexico, which lies behind the church of El Carmen, far from the main plaza, was, two centuries ago, inhabited by sober and prosperous people, languid, because they were comfortable; of the wealthy class, so numerous in New Spain, living quietly and decently in the peaceful monotony of their home, until roused to terror almost frenzied, by a visitation of ghastly and horrid nature.

The most pretentious house in the street was that built by one Tristan Alzures, for whom the thoroughfare was named; a man whose business energy and integrity had brought him great wealth, and whose charities and benevolence had earned him a reputation of almost saintly goodness. So much may be inferred from the fact that even in this world, where deeds of goodness are not often recognized, Don Tristan Alzures had been rewarded. Honors and distinctions lauded upon him; the ground whereon his home was built had been gifted to him, although wealthy as he was, by the municipality, in public recognition of his spirit of enterprise and generous deeds.

But neither fame nor merit can give immortality, and so Don Tristan died; but died in all the sweet fragrance of sanctity, mourned ostentatiously by guilds and associates, lamented selfishly by those to whom he had been a benefactor, and even regretted sincerely and disinterestedly by one—his son and successor, another Tristan.

The son succeeded to all his father's belongings, except his reputation; that is not hereditary, any more than ability or worth. And Tristan the younger was a different sort of person from his father; painted in neutral colors, it might be said. Yet under his quiet demeanor, and slow, almost dull speech, was a nature strong, fearless, and true, and a latent energy and force of great momentum. He was not an enthusiast, this son of the dead rich man, and he took life very quietly. For some weeks, even months, after his father's demise, his daily existence was an unvarying routine. He arose early, took a cold bath that is in Mexico up to the present day the surest remedy against rheumatism, pneumonia, typhus, and all the rapacious attendants on the dreadful miasmas arising from bad drainage. After the morning chocolate, young Alzures went to the great counting-house, and there passed the day with only a brief interval at the midday meal. He took no siesta, and his mourning garb prevented him from seeking social distractions, if he had felt so inclined: thus, returning home in the evening, as soon as he had ate, he went to bed.

Taken into consideration this methodical and secluded life, and add that young Alzures's servants felt for him a respect almost equivalent to awe, and far too intense to permit them to call his attention to gossip, and good reason appears why Tristan, in his solitary home, should not have heard or known of the direful rumors afloat in the barrio, and the all too practical effects resulting from it. His first knowledge of the existing condition of affairs came from his one intimate friend, Marcial Rasgón, a young man of about his own age, and, as might be inferred, a happy and vivacious character—almost the opposite in every respect of Tristan. In the great sala, furnished with richness, sumptuous, indeed, but stiff and somewhat forbidding, like all the rooms fitted after the constrained style of the times, Rasgón sat awaiting his friend one afternoon when Tristan reached the house.

"Oh man! I'm happy to see you!" cried the host,

embracing his guest after the fashion of the land, and prolonging the warm-hearted palmadita, or pat upon the back, with which the greeting emphasized. And Tristan led the way to the dining-room where a great buffet was set in dreary splendor for one, and clapped his hands till half a score of servants came running to lay a place setting for young Rasgón.

But the visitor was ill at ease. He had been waiting long for Tristan, who had not come in till dusk; and, although inside the grated, unglazed windows, the wickets were closed in the massive wooden shutters, and the heavy damask curtains covered the windows, a glimpse of the outside world was had now and then, as a servant opened a door coming from the patio, and that glimpse showed a sky already purple-dark, and powdered thick with stars. No longer could Rasgón restrain his uneasiness. He rose, and picked up his wide brimmed hat.

"I will see you again on Sunday, Tristan."

Alzures looked over at his guest with wondering eyes. "Ay Dios! On Sunday then! And why are you leaving now? You've only been here a short quarter of an hour -- and for the first time in weeks. You have not visited me since my father's funeral."

"Now, as to that," said Rasgón, holding up his head with the frankness and the spirit of a man justified, "as to that, you must know I had to go just at that time to Vera Cruz on matters of importance, and I came back only a week ago."

"A week!" said Tristan in honest indignation, "a week! Weren't we supposed to be together every day, and all day long? No doubt I am dull company, unfit for cheerful companions, and unsightly, moreover, in this"—he touched his black mourning garb—"still one expects a little sympathy from one's friends."

"Now hear me, Tristan," said Marcial Rasgón, who was moved by the other's melancholy bitter tone; "You didn't know that is the case, can't you trust me? But all day long you are absorbed in your affairs, and at night—well, the fact is, at night I am afraid to come here."

"Afraid!" echoed Alzures, sorely perplexed. "Why, man, in all Mexico there is no safer street than this one. Now, if it were the street of Don Juan Manuel! There, I grant you should be afraid, where a person is mugged every night in the week, and twice on Sunday! But the criminals never have come here."

"Nor do I fear them," responded Rasgón, waxing sullen at what he deemed his friend's willful misapprehension. "You know I am no coward. I think I proved that well when our party was held up by bandits at the Llanos of Apam, and again in more than one gun fight. But it is permitted for the bravest of men to be afraid of a ghost."

"A ghost! My God! What ghost are you talking about? I have not heard of one."

And now it was Rasgón's turn to look amazed. "You're joking, Tristan! You are not a comedian. But, I forgot. You are near sighted—a myopic—yes, and at the time your get up in the morning, you would not be able to see anything."

"For weeks past, this area has been the theatre of a ghastly scene. Every night, soon after the call to vespers— that mournful bell that, summoning us to pray for the departed, reminds us that we too are mortal—at that hour, then, as if evoked by the prayers from a grave where he can not rest, a phantom appears—a spirit—what shall I say? Something frightful to behold, chilling the blood of all who see it. And from that hour till midnight that disembodied, dreadful specter traverses this street, and no one dares to meet it. Why, haven't you heard about it when you go to church?—But no! You only hear the mass, where requiems are sung for your father's soul. Here, not a fortnight since, our good curate of El Carmen came into this street with all the holy paraphernalia, to exorcise and to ban the Horror. But all his invocations were in vain. There is no doubt, he says, that some sin against the Holy Church in life has put this tortured soul beyond the reach of the church's offices, and he can tell his woe and put off his burden only through the medium of some fellow sinner, who shall dare challenge his distress. To such a one, the priest promises absolute indulgence, for the good work he shall do, both in relieving a soul in torment, and in bringing prosperity back to this barrio. Why, Tristan, my friend, every one who can move from here has gone, from the terror of the specter. There are palms tied on the window-bars of the houses, and you know that before, not a house was for rent on street."

Muttering some expressions of surprise, but less emphatic than Rasgón thought the occasion demanded, young Alzures got his coat and hat, and offered to accompany his friend to his home. Upon returning, he walked slowly back and forth the length of the street. He had resolved to meet the Phantom, and to challenge the Horror. It was not that he was free from superstitious fears. The training of the times, subject to the dark and bloody rule of the Inquisition in Mexico, and the traditions of Aztec origin, were safe to nourish and inculcate such beliefs. But the watchword of life to Tristan Alzures was DUTY. He felt it his duty here to brave the unknown terror, and his decision was simply and promptly taken.

He was turning for the second time from the end of the street, when at its extreme limit he saw—what? A Something—a shapeless form; and his flesh seemed to turn to living ice, his tongue stuck to the roof of his mouth, and he stood sinking, nerveless, as the Thing came straight toward him. It moved with a slow, noiseless glide, and as it came nearer, it took the semblance of a man, still, intangible as a cloud, though definite in form. It would have passed the young man, shrinking against the wall, but with one mighty, supreme effort, he put out his hand, and gasped:

"Stay! What and who are you?"

The specter paused on the instant. A close observer, calm of pulse and unafraid, would have said that its attitude bespoke something of wistfulness, of hesitancy, of pity. But it spoke no word, only drew a long, shuddering sigh, like the last breath of life.

Tristan gained courage as he waited, and again he invoked the apparition to utterance. "Speak! What is your burden? What crime committed in life entails upon you to unrest after death?" Still again he questioned, but he could get the Thing to answer other than a long, sobbing sigh.

But the third time, the specter spoke: "Unhappy, you who must suffer the penalty of another's sin! Would any other have dared to help me! It may be that this shall enter into my punishment. To compass my punishment, this you shall do tonight. Go to your home, and in your bedroom, four paces from your bed, at the left of the big window, lift up the floor tiles, and dig beneath. The box you shall find there, you shall take tomorrow to the archbishop. I will tell him in his dreams tonight that you are coming. And with this, you will free my soul from torment. May God be with you now, and comfort you in the sore affliction before you. Farewell! Farewell! Farewell!"

Then, silently as it had come, and swiftly, the shrouded figure faded away before the eyes of Tristan, who was left cold and rigid by the ominous weight of its words. The gist of its instructions could hardly leave a doubt in the mind of the young man that he had been speaking to the shade of his father. And what a dreadful crime and suffering, of ruin and disgrace perhaps, was foretold by the words he had just heard.

Dismayed and sorrowful, Tristan turned towards his home, and once within his own room—the same that his father had once occupied—he set himself resolutely to work to obey the command he had received. Indeed, and in good truth, when he had made in the spot indicated an excavation some four feet in depth, his pick struck hard metal, and he lifted out a small box, so heavily bound in iron that the wood barely showed through its interstices.

Early in the morning, after a sleepless night, Tristan left with the coffer to the residence of the archbishop.

"His Reverence has just been asking if a man with a box had not come," said the door-porter in the great arched zaguán. And Tristan's heart grew faint, for against the evidence of his senses, he had hoped his vision might have proven a dream, and that the finding of the box was but a coincidence.

The Archbishop of that time was a saintly old man, the sincerity confirmed by his holy, charitable life. He listened to Tristan's story with infinite nostalgia, for the young man's grave, consistent character commanded all his esteem, while in his heart of hearts the ecclesiastic had never liked Alzures the elder.

"Leave the coffer with me," the old man said at last; "God knows what awful secret it holds within! And yet, my son, it may be that we worry over nothing. Perhaps this is no more serious than some forgotten bequest for charitable deeds, or provisions for saying additional masses for your father's soul. I will tell you soon."

When Tristan had left him alone, not all the Archbishop's efforts sufficed to open the box. On it was visible neither lock nor hinges, and in the ornate decoration of iron with which it was encased, there appeared no variation to determine an aperture. It was only when the Archbishop, fatigued and discouraged by the futility of his efforts, leaned upon it with a sigh, that some refractory spring was loosened by the pressure, and the corner slipped, grating back. That iron-bound case held another, lighter, box, and within the second receptacle was but papers. The first was a formidable-looking document, written on thick parchment-like paper, and heavily sealed with the Alzures seal. The inscription it bore was this:

"TO HIM WHO SHALL BE ARCHBISHOP WHEN THIS IS FOUND."

The cleric broke the seal.

"I am three times a hypocrite," the contents ran, written in the elegant, formal characters of the Spanish scribe, "not content with usurping among my brother sinners a reputation for goodness and honesty most undeserved, I die professing the utmost obedience and devotion to the church, the while I obtain her blessing and absolution by false pretense, feigning to have confessed devoutly all my sins, and claiming forgiveness for them. Let me tell here the truth: I follow this faithless course from fear and shame to meet the just disgrace of my fellow-citizens, whose esteem and favors I have so long enjoyed, rather than from apprehension that mother church might refuse to pardon my sin. This is the story of my evil doing: Fifteen years ago I found in danger of immediate destruction the business I had built up with laborious care and patient attention. Excessive, extra taxes had just been imposed upon commerce; family demands were making heavy encroachments on my resources, and two successive ships, dispatched with goods for me from Spain, had gone down at sea, or fallen prey to pirates. I had no friends or family from whom I could bring myself to ask assistance, and I was sunk in despair. At the very climax of my tribulation, when all seemed hopelessly dark, and another week should bring full ruin on me, in the falling due of a tremendous debt I had no means to pay—at this moment of stress came to Mexico City, at once for pleasure and business, my old-time friend, Fernando Gómez, of Guanajuato. The yield of his mines had brought him fabulous wealth, and I might have asked him for help to tide over the disaster threatening me. But Gómez was a cautious man, a miser almost, and I believe that at the first hint of my distress he would have turned his back upon me. I gave him hospitality in my house, and all was well between us. Gómez had brought gold with him from Guanajuato, and letters of credit. He duly cashed them all, and brought the treasure home to my house, and hid it in the traveling chest he had brought. `We are two rich men together,' he said to me often, `each so rich that neither need fear the other will rob him.' Perhaps that speech awoke the devil in my heart. Gómez had been with me three days; his money was all collected, and on the next day he would begin to pay it out for certain investments. I formed a black resolve to murder Gómez, and all the conditions were in my favor. He had a tryst that night that he wished to conceal, for he passed in the world for a sort of second St. Anthony.

"His tryst was for three nights in succession, during the

absence of certain parties from Mexico City, and his plan was to go out early in the evening, and return to my house at an advanced hour, by means of a secret side-door, unknown to the servants, using the same means of egress to go out about his business during the day. Therefore he mentioned before the servants that he was going to Texcoco for a few days, and at night I ushered him to the door with all the ceremony of the occasion, in view of three or four of my people. At four o'clock in the morning he scratched at the side door, where I awaited him, and half an hour later he was sleeping soundly. All was silent. The servants were at rest in their own quarters, and my wife and child were at the hacienda. I took a dagger of finest temper, and, bending over Gómez I buried it in his heart.   I carried his body to the room—itself a secret chamber—where I opened the secret door, and then returned to the scene of my crime, and spent the remaining hours before my usual time of arising in removing the any traces of my crime, and in transferring Gómez' money to my own strong box. The following night I buried the body under the floor of the room where it was hidden. I paid my debts and established my business once more on a substantial basis. Gómez' disappearance attracted little notice—these things are not so uncommon here among us. I myself went before the Mayor of the City to ask an investigation, but what could the Mayer do? I and my servants testified he had left us to go to

Texcoco. At Texcoco he had never arrived. It was easy to conclude that his boatmen killed him for his jewels, throwing his body into the wide lagoon? As for his family in Guanajuato, perhaps his heirs were content not to find him. From that day on I prospered, as all the city knows. But, although I die with falsehood and cowardice adding to the burden of sin already resting on my soul, I can but make provision for the ultimate disclosing of the truth, that atonement and restitution may be made. As I die a traitor to my church, perhaps that church's benediction will give no rest to my soul, and I leave herein a gateway of escape from the torments of hell, praying that my earthly fellows who judge me, that they spare insomuch my dear son Tristan, who of all this he knows nothing, and is blameless; and who is moreover, of another fiber than mine.

—TRISTAN ALZURES THE FATHER."

The good Archbishop read this with horror and dismay. There mingled in his mind a shocked distress for the fate of Gómez of Guanajuato, cut off from life and repentance in the midst of his sins; mixed censure and compassion for the dead murderer; and, stronger than all beside, a tender, yearning pity for young Tristan, the guiltless son of so deeply criminal father.

"And Tristan the son is good and noble," thought the

Archbishop; "he is honest, true, and very charitable. In his hands this ill-gotten wealth will do nothing but good. Wherefore disgrace the lad and shame his father's memory, being the case now that nothing good can result from so doing? Instead will I confer with Tristancito, for the disinterment of Gómez, whose bones should lie in consecrated ground. With this, Tristan will give generously from his wealth for masses for the dead—all hapless both—and a liberal portion monthly to the poor. Since the will of the dead has brought this to my knowledge, surely it is fitting that I arbitrate upon it."

But, even while the good old cleric, full of charity for the sins of his kind, full of love and mercy for the sinful dead, and great with compassion to the living sufferers—while, then, the good Archbishop pondered how best to spare the living with never a wrong to the dead—there came at his door a loud, imperious knocking, and it opened to the guards of the Inquisitor-General of Mexico, to whom the door porter had hastened to babble of his master's dream, and its strange complementary sequel.

"His worship demands the coffer and its contents," said the grim official in command.

There was nothing to be said. The good Archbishop, beloved through he was of the people—indeed, not improbably because of the affection commanded by his gentle and upright character—found small favor with the Tribunal of the Inquisition. To that court was carried the appeal of the dead Tristan Alzures, and the verdict passed upon the matter may be judged by the occurrences of the following day.

Early in the forenoon a band of workmen entered the Callejón de Alzures, and, halting in front of the house for whose master the street was named, they proceeded to erect before it's a great gallows-tree, in such manner that the horrid fruit it should bear would hang in front of the open door. Then came a group of the peons employed about the graveyard; they bore a corpse, the which, it was plain to see, had just been disinterred; and, with brutal roughness and ignominious words, they suspended it from the gallows. The while a robust monk, barefoot and clad in frock of coarsest sackcloth, stood before the house, and related, in sonorous tones, the details of Alzures' crime. It goes without saying that the rabble gathered about, along with some high-ranking individuals. All confessed to sensations of horror and distress incommensurate with the feeling, intense though it might be, inspired by the facts as made known. None could explain the strange and powerful oppression until, as the body swayed and turned in the wind, some one caught sight of a silver crucifix that hung form the straining neck, and then the cry went up from all that great assemblage: "The Ghost! The phantom that has haunted the street! The ghost was

Alzures!" Soon the great zaguán of the Alzures' mansion opened and from it a funeral procession, rich with all the pomp and display of a church burial, accompanied by a priest and layman. It moved in slow procession to the Cathedral, whereby, after imposing ceremonies, to the graveyard; and there was buried the mortal parts of Gómez of Guanajuato, exhumed in the secret chamber of the Alzures mansion, in accordance with the slayer's directions.

The ancient chronicles avow that the bodies of both Alzures and Gómez, notwithstanding the long period of the latter's burial, were fresh and well-preserved as the newly dead. The body of Alzures hung for twenty-four hours upon the gallows, and was then buried at the stake at the Quemadero, or place of execution by fire, where is at present the lovely Alameda.

Tristan Alzures the younger entered the priesthood, and, it may be known without saying, the immense estates of his inheritance were confiscated by the Inquisition. The street of the Alzures was renamed "The Street of the Dead Man," and to this day it is called the El Callejón del Muerto.

Y. H. ADDIS.   CITY OF MEXICO, July, 1887.

A Mexican Lucrece

The Tragic Legend of the Street of the Jewel
By Yda Addis
Appeared in *The Argonaut*, August 20, 1887

The street was named thus many and many year ago, when the City of Mexico as yet was young. The City of Mexico thus named and known; for the Great Tenochtitlan—the Town of the Snake and the Cactus—had stood on the same site, how long before, there is no man can tell. But the happenings to be recited in the present tale befell after the Conquistadores had built, on the spot whence they had razed the Aztec city, the capital of New Spain, and had enrooted in the new soil as many as they might of the customs of their native land, overlaying the half-barbaric manners of the times with what pomp and luxury of life they could command, all heedless that, giving as they did to Mexico all they enjoyed in Spain, all still fell far short, in many chief respects, of the civilization and advancement whose tokens they swept away from the conquered land. But the haughty Spanish spirit was given to no reflections so little complacent, and the social and political fiats were all modeled on the plan of those of other lands across the seas. The vice-regal circle at Mexico reproduced in little the sumptuous glitter and glory of the Spanish court, with its pomp, and form, and the elaborate ceremony; and more than in little it copied, too, the corrupt and profligate life of the old world. The nobles were gay, and—barring external pretensions—godless; their splendor flouted back his rays to the sun; and the poor here as elsewhere, ashamed and shrinking in their rags, shunning the too penetrating, too disclosing light of day. Between the two was a great middle class, here as everywhere the hope and the salvation of the country, free from the privations and sufferings that inevitably harden and degrade the very poor, and, from inclination as well as from questions of caste, avoiding the temptations and the responsibilities of the higher rank.

Of this intermediate grade were Gaspar Villareal and his wife, Violante Armejo. Gaspar was of good, although not noble, family, and he had inherited a patrimony sufficient to maintain a moderate family, free from the necessity of labor. He was an intelligent and clever man, who might have taken office, and therein found preferment, if he had so elected. But something of a philosopher he was, and seeing clearly through the flimsy shams of attraction in such a life, he chose to live own, serene and apart. It would have been hard to find a fitter mate for Villareal than his wife, Violante. She was of wondrous beauty, and when she came to the city from her clear-aired mountain home, and learned what unclean thoughts, and schemes, and passions seethed through the general life of the day, she was fain to turn aside and bury that extreme loveliness, as in a convent, behind the jalousies of the little home to which her husband brought her.

In those days, ere the vandal axe of the conqueror had ravaged the works of God from the face of the earth, as it had already destroyed the works of man, the whole Valley of Mexico, now flat and bare of woodland, was timbered thickly throughout; and in a clump of noble cottonwood trees, a league away from the city, Gaspar had made his home. A modest place it was, supplied, indeed, with all the comforts known to that day and section, but owning little of luxury. It was a shrine of heaven, however, to the loving pair. In the little garden they sat in converse or woke the tones of the young wife's guitar, or read from old-world poets, being more studiously inclined than the major part of their neighbors of that day and generation. And husband and wife were happy, loving, and knowing no doubt of one another.

Along the highway that skirted this little Eden rode one fine day Diego de Fajardo, a young gallant and noble, newly arrived from Spain. Returning from the chase, the pangs of thirst beset him on the way, and chance, or fate—it could never have been Providence—led him to draw rein and check his mare Xeres at the zaguán door of Villareal, and ask a draught of water from the mozo at the door. It was toward the decline of the day, and Violante sat in the corridor looking upon the garden, and watched the linnets stealing apricots from the trees. She heard the young voice at the doorway, and the merest bend of her head would have shown her the form of the handsome cavalier, yet she moved not a hair's breath. What to her was the semblance of gay gentlemen, living here in her cottage, far retired from the alien intrigues of the court? For her there was but one man on earth worth bending aside to see, and he was her own true husband. But the claim of hospitality was quite another thing. She called to the mozo as he passed, doffing his hat of straw, and bearing to the stranger a jácara of water.

"Go put away the gourd, Joaquín," she said, "and bring from the sala—see, here are the keys—thy master's cup of silver, and a crystal cup on a tray with a flask of wine. From the voice of the stranger yonder, he should be a person of quality, and it ill beseems that such go from thy master's house with only the comfort of a meager cup of water." And the servant did her bidding, and, proud of the quality of hospitality dispensed by his patrons, he explained to the young cavalier the reason of the change in his refreshment.

The etiquette of the day was imperative and cumbrous, and to Diego de Fajardo, living in the atmosphere of most rigorous conventionality, it seemed that he would do a churlish thing did he ride away without making his acknowledgements to the mistress of the house in person. His conception of her—formed, as we always imagine the personality of an unknown person, instantly and unconsciously, in vagueness—was that of an elderly woman. The servant's term "la niña" told him nothing, for in Mexico of that day, as still at the present, that infantile phrase was applied to the babe in arms, or indifferently to the dame of ninety years. De Fajardo tossed his bridle rein to the man, and passed into the garden. Violante still sat in her hammock garbed in spotless white raiment, with her long satin braids fraying against the tiles of the corridor floor as she swung slightly, impelled by one delicate foot. The plumes of the gallant's broad-brimmed hat trembled as if wind-shaken, as it hung at his side, and almost fell from his hand. The usual glib fluency of his speech hushed in his throat, and he could not utter the compliment of thanks he had come to speak. He stammered out some incoherent phrases, and bowed himself away. His spasm of modesty, however, was only temporary, and he had ridden not half a league before the old Adam in his nature repented bitterly of his sensibility, and he turned about and rode back to the thickets around the little *quinta*, when he could perceive the graceful form of Violante moving about her abode.

These times were not the times of pretty morals. The Spaniards of that regime were dissolute and profligate to the last degree, and by them women were regarded simply as a quarry to be run down for passing amusement. No thought, then, of honor, duty, or responsibility deterred Diego de Fajardo from his pursuit of the wife of Gaspar Villareal. His accustomed interests failed him under the overwhelming force of this new passion, which was a veritable infatuation; for no other woman had attracted him as did this one. He renounced his usual avocations, and gave himself up wholly to the one purpose. But the conditions were unfavorable to his wishes. Content and happy in the company of each other, and with no sordid demands of necessity to separate them, the Villareals were never long apart, and de Fajardo found no opportunity to approach Violante out of her husband's presence. That his advances might be repulsed, he never dreamed. Rich, young, and noble, gifted with many charms of person and manner, and disillusioned of woman's loyalty and virtue by many facile conquest among the complaisant ladies of the court, it never occurred to him that other types of women still existed, not that love for another might prove a mightier safeguard for a woman than any consideration of personal dignity or safety. Therefore, on every day that he rode out toward the home of Villareal, he rode as one secure of conquest, were the lists but open. But many and many a day found his quest fruitless. Gaspar Villareal was ever at the *quinta*, held there, not by bonds of suspicion but by ties of affection; until at last, approaching the house near nightfall, the anxious would-be wooer saw the husband come forth, and, taking saddle, ride toward the city.

Now that the moment had come, he could scarce believe in his good fortune. Exultant, eager, confident, he threw himself upon his knees before Violante, as the usage of the times demanded, and poured forth a flood of eloquent protestations of devotion.

Violante smiled at his ardor.

"But you have chosen wrongly. These little comedies are amusing, that I grant you. But, for their participation, one needs not only the court training but the leisure needful for practice. You were mistaken, caballero, to think to find a competent person in me—a humble villager from the mountains."

As in duty bound, Diego de Fajardo swore his sincerity by the souls of saints and disciples; and in his tremulous speech, for all its exaggerations, rang the convincing tones of a genuine passion. But its discovery held no softening influence over Violante—all the contrary. When de Fajardo had first rushed into her presence, her displeasure had been tempered by an amused endurance, supposing that this was but the perfunctory impromptu profession of some court gallant, determined to slight no opportunity to practice his fascinations. But she now perceived that a deeper motive lay beneath his behavior, prompted by deliberate intention, it was evident; and all her dignity of self-respect and loyal self-consecration rose up in arms with mighty indignation, and found utterance in words so earnest, so full of scorn, so bitterly trenchant, that the young man before her shrank and cowered as if touched by the ignominy of the lash.

So clear and logical were the words of Violante, so true and just were her expressed convictions, that the notes of her voice fell cold and hard as hail on the flame of Diego's ardor, and dispelled the delirium in which he was wrapped by her presence. For the first time, he was beheld of his own eyes by the true light. The glamour of his light loves and his adventures fell away like a mantle, and he saw his own conduct in all its hideous nakedness and viewed himself—Diego de Fajardo, of enviable rank and station, as he had considered, a personage, a paragon his true charter—despoiler of homes, and so a false friend, a traitor; an intriguer for contemptible results, a libertine whose pursuits had not the extenuation that might be offered by the interest of a real passion. Calmed, disconcerted, abashed, trembling with mortification and the weakness of reaction from the frenzy that had possessed him, he stumbled to his feet, and left the presence of Violante, and hurried homewards, another man than when he rode out thither.

Mistaken as had been its manifestations, this was a true love that had awakened in his bosom, and it brought this resolution—henceforth the paths wherein he had walked would be no longer charming, but loathsome.

As for Violante a shock of horror possessed her. She had known of the evil in the world, with sufficient detail and clearness, as needs a woman must in that day and generation, however innocent; but an abstract knowledge of evil is a very different thing to a woman from that which surges about herself, creeps to her feet and scorches them, laps her garments, and leaves its sear upon them. She was stunned, she was all aquiver with burning recoil and pain, she was wretchedly instinct with a sense of stain and pollution, as if she were to blame for the sin of another; as if some occult, hitherto undiscovered quality in herself had been the spring of de Fajardo's conduct.

She was fleeing to her chamber to seek her rosary, to cool her throbbing brow with the touch of holy water, when her foot struck an object lying near her. Her glance turned upon it—it sparkled. She stooped and took it into her hand. It was a bracelet—a splendid jewel, rich with incrustations; and on its inner surface, newly engraved, her own name "Violante," close beside the coronet and arms of de Fajardo.

This was a fresh blow to her. In the story it told of her suitor's conviction of success she seemed to feel herself by force compelled to acquiescence, and her sensations were as if de Fajardo had, in spite of herself, embraced her.

As she stood there with the jewel in her hand, a step sounded behind her; she turned. There stood her husband. Villareal, returning sooner than he expected, had been struck with horror on nearing his home to see a man rush from its gateway, spring into saddle, and ride away so madly that the husband, as he passed, could neither stop nor hail him, nor even see his countenance. Gaspar had hastened, fearing to meet in his home-nest he knew not what evidence of deeds of ghastly violence. He found his wife overwhelmed with agitation—surely pallor and trembling are the signs of a guilty conscience—and in her hand a regal jewel, like none that he could give her.

Gaspar Villareal was a man of mighty and impetuous passions. If his faith in Violante had been absolute, he believed in no other woman, and the merest suggestion sufficed to create a reaction in his jealous nature. As the fond wife turned to meet him, secure in the knowledge of her own unwavering loyalty, and thinking to find her natural refuge from the shame and indignation that had distressed her—as she joyfully sprang toward him, he lifted a hand toward heaven, a if in accusation or invocation, and in it glittered somewhat that seemed to mock the bauble in the hand of Violante—and something that—was it by analogy?—was gleaming from her bosom as she sank to the floor, gasping. Gaspar Villareal stood gazing down upon her. A crimson current bubbled from her breast, over her spotless draperies, and crept across the tiles till it laved the gleaming bracelet still grasped in her stiffening, nerveless fingers, and dimmed its sumptuous brilliance. Villareal snatched that ill-omened token from the dead woman with a certain ferocious, vindictive jealousy, and examined it for a trace of his enemy.

"Diego de Fajardo!" he cried, and seemed to find an added pang in the thought that his undoing was the work of this famous gallant, with whose adventures the city was ever ringing. Then he plucked the dagger from that bleeding freezing bosom, and fled along the causeway toward the city.

Diego de Fajardo had passed a dreadful, solemn night of introspection and self-arraignment, and its issue had been a resolution to retire from the world and enter the cloister, now that he was confronted with the spectres of his sins, and the one true love of his lifetime—a love that might have redeemed him to uses good and lofty, but that its hopelessness mocked him.

Resolved, however, to lapse no more into his old-time degradation, he fell at last asleep exhausted, but was all too soon awakened by his confidential servant, trembling like the palsied, and with a white, scared countenance.

"Señor, a strange and awful thing has happened. Will it please your worship to dress and descend to the zaguán as speedily as may be? The people fear to change aught till you have seen. Perhaps you can understand it."

Aye, aye! too well, indeed, Diego de Fajardo understood the sight that met his eyes when he reached the great arched street entrance. Near by, on the cold stone flags of the pavement, Gaspar Villareal lay rigid, his garments soaked in the life blood that had welled from his lips and clotted in a pool beside him.

And high beside the great bronze knocker on the massive door of de Fajardo's mansion hung a strange and awful object—a splendid diamond bracelet, whose gems flashed here and there through their ensanguined coating, suspended on a blood-stained dagger that had been driven into the oaken panels with a mighty blow of despair and agony.

Y. H. Addis.   August, 1887.

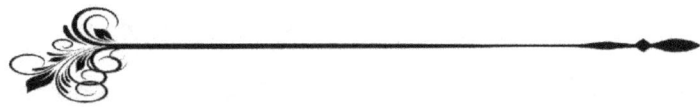

The Love-Lorn Suicide

A Spanish Legend.
By
Yda Addis
Appeared in *The Argonaut* June 20, 1888

There is no doubt that Perico's want of common sense brought him very near the grade of the tailed animals; from childhood up he gave clear proofs of this fact. His mother was wont to reproach him with being "a brute-beast," and certainly that good lady, who was a devotee, never accused herself, in the confessional, of bearing false witness against her offspring. When Perico, playing with other children, fell into difficulties with them, but pounded his own pate until he saw stars enough for a dozen skies. More than once the Señor Cura had said of him: "That boy has a fiendish tendency toward suicide, and it will be a miracle if he does not give his family a fine fright one of these days."

Perico had become a young man, but a bigger fool than ever, when he gave another proof that the inclination of which the Cura spoke had increased, instead of diminishing. The Señor Cura, Perico, and others of the villagers were sitting under a tree in the church-yard, awaiting the hour of mass, when there passed by Robustiana, who was a strapping wench, six fingers above water-mark (the standard of proper height for women is five feet); she carried her water-jar upon her head, and was singing:

"I am not afraid of Death, though he look me in the eyes;
For without the leave of God, there is not a soul that dies!"

"Now, those lines," said the Señor Cura to Robustiana, "are such as you ought to sing, instead of the foolish and shameless verses you learn from your sweethearts."

"Well, that snatch," said Perico, "seems to me about the most foolish of any, saving your presence, Señor Cura."

"And why, then?"

"Because it says that no one can die without the leave of God."

"And that is a truth as big as a church!"

"Truth, nothing! Suppose I take a notion to kill myself; I would do it without the permission of God, surely!"

"No, not unless it were His will that you should kill yourself. Hush, boy! don't talk like a fool! God has power over the arms and the weapons of men, and your poor feeble resolves are as naught, as against His holy will!"

Perico, stubborn and pig-headed, was about to reply, when the sexton rang the first bell for mass, and the Señor Cura hurried away to don his vestments.

Perico had neither father nor mother, nor little dog to bark at him. His parents, dying, had left him a house; old, to be sure, but comfortable enough, and ample. Besides, a goodly store of furniture, clothing, jewels, wine, grain, and even a bit of money. But Perico, with his countless follies, had run through with all the movables, so that he was left almost with bare walls. And he was very much in love with Robustiana.

He rose one morning in very unpleasant humor, and fell to soliloquizing: "There is no wine in the cellar, nor wheat in the granary. I have no money, and, the truth is, I hate work! What the devil am I going to do when I have nothing to fall dead upon? Hello! I must go slowly there. There's plenty to fall dead on. What's the matter with the pavement under my balcony? Aren't those flags rich enough for any one to fall on, and, shatter the golden bowl, eh? The Cura says no one can kill himself without God's leave. Humph! I'll show the Señor Cura if I have to go begging leave and license for such doings. And Robustiana, who won't ever squeeze my hand, even. She'll see what kind of lad she has flouted! Here goes! Farewell, proud world, I'm going home!" Then he opened the shutters, put his hand on the balcony railing, and—one! two! three! over he went, head foremost.

But luck would have it that the damsel Robustiana was just then passing, and, hearing the noise as the shutters were jerked opened, she looked up in time to see the young man flying through the air, and, spreading her stout arms, she caught him, plump! and, staggering under the weight of him, she sank down to the ground, still holding him, and there she petted and coddled him, until, seeing that he was quite uninjured, she shook him out of his cozy refuge, and walked away, sniffing, not to say snorting, in wrath and disgust.

Now Perico, who had been in the seventh heaven for a few moments, found himself worse off than ever with his sudden repulse by his charmer, and accordingly he nerved himself for desperate deeds as she turned the corner. "Now, what am I going to do? he demanded of himself. "Go up and jump out of the window again? No, that don't work. I can't blow out my brains, for I haven't any pistol, not the good, hard dollars to buy one. Never mind! they shall see! oh, yes! I know what to do! I'll hang myself. I've got it this time!"

He went into the house, and from among his few remaining possessions he hunted out a strong hempen cord, and greased it thoroughly with tallow, so it would run upon itself easily. Then he made a slip-noose on one end, tied the other to a rafter, climbed on a chair, put the noose around his neck, kicked the chair away, and there he hung, making a whirlwind of himself in the air. Perico was very fat—for it is well-known that the way fools fatten is a caution!—and his weight made the roof tremble. The rafters were so old they were nothing but tinder, and presently down came the one to which Perico was swinging, with a rattling, clattering, metallic noise, like that of two hundred thousand devils on horseback.

Perico, who had become senseless, recovered himself in the midst of that noise, which was enough to arouse the dead. He looked around him and saw that the floor of the room was literally carpeted thickly with golden ounces, of the coinage of Charles the Third. It was clear that an enormous sum in ounces had been hidden away above the rafter, which, tiring, no doubt, of that weight which it had borne for years and years without any one coming to its relief, had availed itself of the first opportunity to shake off its load. Perico stacked the money away in a closet which had been too long empty, and notwithstanding that the embrace of the cord had left its reminder upon his neck, he breathed freely for the first time since he had spent the last dollar of the paternal legacy. "Now," he said to himself; "now I am rich, and consequently Robustiana will not consider me ugly."

Was there ever anything more absurd than this inference that money of the date of Charles the Third, or any other coinage, would influence a woman's regard for a man?

Oh! it is quite evident that Perico was a great fool.

Now that this adorer had fortified himself with new hope, he paid more assiduous court to Robustiana. The mother of the girl was not disinclined to constitute herself his advocate, but it did try her patience and good feeling that he would persist in planting himself under their windows, at about fifteen hundred o'clock at night, scraping a guitar, and singing in his calf's voice sweet ditties like the following:

"If, instead of blooming roses,

Weeds were growing on your face,

I'd be first to browse upon them

Of all donkeys in the place!"

Or this other delicate, sentimental lay:

"Should your mother hear me singing,

And `What's that?' she should be saying,

Answer he, `Oh, that is nothing

But a donkey that is braying!'"

"Daughter of mine!" then would exclaim the mother; "why don't you agree to marry that young man, and put him out of his misery?"

"Oh, yes!" returned the amiable daughter; "and the first fine day going I might be left a widow."

"Oh, no! he has lost his craze for killing himself."

"Now that may be, too. But he is such a fool, that that is enough to kill him." So that Perico had no reward for his gallantries but to hear from within the house the scolding voices of the women, and the barking of their fierce dog Rasgabrazos, who raged as if a whole band of thieves were prowling near; and, at last, one night the disdainful maiden slyly set the door ajar, and out leaped Rasgabrazos. Perico turned to flee. In retreat he was naturally in part unguarded, and the teeth of the dog met in the redundancy of his flesh—but it were only kind to draw a veil over the sad occurrence.

This mishap made poor Perico desperate, and all the old dark designs and intentions beset him.

"It is clear that Robustiana loves me not," he muttered; "and of what use are all the yellow-boys in the closet yonder, if so be it that the women, being the same thing as the devil, flee from the money, because a cross is marked on it? Oh-h-h, no! I'll settle it this time! No lack of a pistol, now. And I'll lift it up like a gentleman, and this will be a question of blood, and bones, and brains scattered about till all these folks will learn to respect and admire me for my courage. And we'll see, too, if I have to memorialize heaven and take out a permit to kill myself!"

He waited until night, that the report of the shot might sound louder in the silence, and then, cocking the pistol, he lifted it to his temple, and had all but fired it, when suddenly—

"I'd better see that no one is near enough to rush in and find me still breathing and revive me, so that I shall waste my powder," he said to himself. So he stepped into the balcony of the adjacent room, and carefully scanned the street. Satisfied of the absence of possible intermeddlers, he returned and took up the pistol, but hesitated a short time, to see if he could recall some flowery verses he had endeavored to compose in honor of Robustiana.

"But, after all, what use?" he said, "she never would listen to them." Pressing the muzzle of the weapon tightly against his forehead, he discharged it, and tumbled to the floor instantly.

But—where were the bones, where the blood, the ghastly scattered brains? There was only a shower of bits of plaster, and scraps of wood and iron. The pistol had burst in the hand of Sir Perico, and a sprained finger and a slight contusion were the only personal damages sustained by the hero. He jumped to his feet and rushed in search of another pistol; but, reaching the other room, the sight there gave him pause!

There, on the floor, were hats and cloaks, a dagger, a crowbar, and several other tools, and the door of the closet stood open, while a capacious bag lay on the floor before it, and the flutter of garments retreating through the window showed the means of ingress of the robbers.

"Well! well!" said Perico; 'this is entertaining! If I had been a moment later about shooting and frightening off those fellows I'd have been left here with a broken pistol, a lump on my forehead, and not a *cuarto* to give a blind man to pray for me! Why, this is almost enough to make a man shoot himself!"

By this time the neighbors had gathered to the sound of the shot, and Perico, finding the conditions scarcely auspicious for the carrying out of his projects, was under the necessity of suspending operations till a more fitting moment.

And with all this he continued more in love with Robustiana than ever. So much so, indeed, that that same night he betook himself again beneath her windows, unheeding his past experience there; and once again the callous-hearted maiden let loose fierce Rasgabrazos, and that animal, having no sense of the proprieties, did then so rend and tear the raiment of Perico, that the poor youth soon found himself in a state wherein he might have served as model for those artists who disdain the hampering of drapery. And to cap the climax, that cruel Robustiana came to the window with a candle, and gazed upon the sorry plight of her victim. It is true that she called off Rasgabrazos, and even feigned to whip him, with a fine show of indignation, and the next morning she informed her mother point-blank of her intention to marry Perico. But the youth knew naught of the resolution to which his charmer had been inspired by his graceful port and comeliness, and it seemed to him that if the first indignity that the sportive Robustiana had put upon him had moved him to a pistol-shot, the second called for his riddling with the balls of a whole battery. He pondered long and gloomily upon the best means of carrying his resolve into execution, and at last conceived a plan which did honor to his fertility of resource.

"I will hang myself from a tree," was his stern resolution; "and, lest the rope should break, I will shoot myself through the head as I swing off to waltz on nothing; lest the pistol fail me, I will eat a box of phosphorus-matches; and, lest they should not be strong enough to take the effect I wish, the tree from which I hang myself shall be one leaning over the water. Now the Señor Cura shall see how about doing with one's life as one pleases."

Thus saying, he provided himself with a strong rope, a new pistol, and a big box of fresh matches, and set out for the beach.

At the water's edge there was a tree that, owing to a landslide, leaned out over the water, and to one of its branches Perico tied one end of his strong new rope, in the slip-knot at whose other extreme he put his neck. Then, champing up the contents of the match-box, he swung into the air, discharging the pistol at the same moment.

Splash ! souse ! he went deep into the water. The pistol ball, instead of entering Perico's brain, had simply cut in two his suicidal halter.

The water heaved and boiled as Perico sank into it, but a few moments later a group of fishermen, who had gathered at the sound of the shot, were pulling him out of the sea, almost more dead than alive, and full of water, which the fishermen hastened to expel by most vigorous and heroic treatment. And with the water was ejected the very considerable ration of phosphorus matches Perico had swallowed.

At this came running Robustiana, to whom the tidings had traveled with the accustomed velocity of ill news, and she at once took charge of the patient, and applied an efficacious system of treatment.

A month later this twain were wedded; but before the Cura would pronounce the nuptial blessing, he exacted from Perico an open admission that no one, however determined and resolute, dies unless it is the will of God that he shall die.

It is to be suspected, however, that the priest's alternative was the source of Perico's conviction; for after the ceremony he was heard to mutter: "We'll see about that one of these days, if Robustiana prove cantankerous," and there is no doubt he remained pig-headed as ever.

Y. H. Addis.   CITY OF MEXICO.

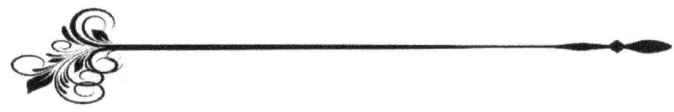

The Street of Don Juan Manuel

A Legend of the City of Mexico
By
Yda Addis
Appeared in *The Argonaut* September 25, 1886

There is in Mexico a street lined by the tallest and most sumptuous buildings, where for years have lived wealthy and prominent merchants. Situated in the most populous, the most central part of the city, it is what we might call an aristocratic street.

Nevertheless, its aspect is dreary by day, and by night lugubrious. The great *zaguán* (street-doors) of ancient carved wood seem the entrances to castles; on the high walls of the buildings are projected, in a most singular manner, the lights and the alternate shades of the street-lamps, and from the Churrigueresque cornices of the balconies phantoms appear to detach themselves, which now blend and hide in the *zaguáns*, now ascend to the roof cornice, and there peep and laugh, showing deformed and fantastic shapes to the people who pass.

Thus to my imagination appeared, one dark night, cold and windy, the Street of Don Juan Manuel. A dear friend of mine was dying that night, and I had to go in search of a good priest, to bestow the last benediction which the Christian craves on the day he departs this life forever.

That night, at intervals, gusts of icy wind blew from off the volcanoes, and now and then great rain-drops fell, which the wind beat and dashed against the dark panes within the balconies; in the whole street there was no living creature but a lean black dog, gnawing a bone thrown out by some servant. The oil-lamps cast shadows rather than light, and the small reddish flame trembled sinisterly in the black tin holder. The watchman slept at the corner, wrapped in his dark-blue mantle, and the echo of footsteps on the flags of the walk resounded along the whole extent of the street at once dismal and majestic, and broke the silence, now and then disturbed also by the croak of some night bird.

This is the historic legend of the Street of Don Juan Manuel:

In the year 1636 the street was not in the condition that wayfarers now behold it. Mexico was already, as it were planned and arranged, by the streets, with few exceptions, were not finished. There were large, fine houses close beside others of poor and defective construction; some had high, well-made fences protecting their gardens, while in others, in the Celada (now the Street of San Bernardo) and in that of which we speak, there were scattered among houses many vacant ground plots, fenced in only with wood, or adobes, or dry thorn bush.

The owner of the houses and grounds in that road was a cavalier called Don Juan Manuel. He was a personage surrounded in all directions by shadows and mysteries which never let him be seen in all the true reality. At night he would enter the palace of the Viceroy, muffled to the eyes in a long black cloak, and there would remain for hours, conversing. None would see him come forth, and some who, from curiosity, watched him go in, declared that before knocking at the private door of the palace, Don Juan Manuel would unmuffle himself, cross himself thrice, and drawing a silver-handled rapier, he would test it, examine its point, and then return it to the sheath. And they who saw this feared that the Viceroy some morning would be found murdered in his bed.

Don Juan Manuel was a very charitable man. It was told of him that he was once visited by a widow who had two charming daughters, young and fair. Don Juan Manuel bestowed five thousand dollars upon each of the girls, and refused even to see them.

Don Juan Manuel was of jealous nature. It was said

that his wife was an illustrious lady of rare beauty, but none had ever seen her, for she remained shut within the house, and only left it to go to mass at five-o'clock of a morning, wrapped in a great black woolen cloak. No one visited the house, and none entered there save the confessor, who now and then went to drink chocolate there after mass.

Don Juan Manuel was brave. One night six robbers set upon him armed with daggers. He drew his sword of the fashion Cid Ruy Díaz, and, setting his back against a *zaguán* door, he let none of them approach him until a patrol came to the rescue, who afterward found the trails of blood made by the assailants, all wounded by the one man.

Don Juan Manuel was not only a good man, but pious; he confessed and took the sacrament every week; he disciplined himself every night at the nearest church; he relieved many of the poor, assisted at the feasts of the Virgin, and paid for tapers and lamps which burned day and night in the churches.

All this was told of Don Juan Manuel, but in reality he was a most mysterious man, of whom it might be assumed that all knew him, and none knew him truly. If asked to describe him, one said he was tall of stature, very straight and stately, with a face pale and almost jaundiced, a thick, black beard, and black, sparkling, deep-set eyes. Others, on the contrary, averred that he was but an ordinary height, with mild and charitable countenance, with eyes expressive and full of sweetness, and only a short mustache. Neither could all agree as to his garb, the best informed concurring in that he wore always black, while others had noted his elegant, hoodless cloaks; but the greatest number were unanimous in saying that at night he might be met in the darkest streets, going in and out of mean-appearing houses, wrapped in a long cloak.

Such was the gossip of the vulgar, which, starting from a foundation of truth, poetizes and reverses things and forms, giving to them the strange, indefinite, or mysterious character which so delights the human imagination. Thus originates the greater part of the legends and traditions of every people.

Time went on and on, and every year added some particular, some new stroke to the character of Don Juan Manuel, as portrayed. Suddenly the cavalier gave himself over completely to religious devotion, and from this he went into a melancholy so black and deep that no one could console him. His cheeks became sunken, a purple circle appeared around his eyes, and his clear, white complexion turned to an opaque, slimy yellow, that at once revealed that he was consumed by terrible physical sufferings, as well as by spiritual illness. For some time Don Juan Manuel remained shut in his house, and none had speech of him. Then, in secret, and with a thousand reserves, the women who were old and devotees declared that Don Juan Manuel had made a compact with the devil, and they blessed themselves and showed the cross for the Evil One. The truth perhaps was that Don Juan Manuel was jealous of his wife, with whom he was madly in love; and as he could not discover nor prove with certainty who it was who robbed him of his honor, he was on the verge of madness from rage and despair.

One night the body of a murdered man was found in that street; but as there was absolutely no police vigilance at that time, and the city was unlighted, and robbers abounded, this misfortune was attributed to them. However, it was remarked that a large sum of money was left in the pockets of the victim. Within a week, another corpse lay in the street now called after Don Juan Manuel. The next day another, and another, and periodically thereafter, others. The city was full of terror—several of the dead men belonging to the best known and most honored families in the city.

The question was, who was the author of those crimes? The vulgar answered that, entirely led away by the devil, to whom he had surrendered his soul on condition of being shown the lover of his wife, Don Juan Manuel went forth every night from his house, closely muffled, with a short dagger in his hand, and when he encountered any man near the house, blinded by jealousy, he would infer that this was one of the many who were resolved to injure his honor, and so asked the other:

"What is the hour?"

"Eleven o'clock," the wayfarer would answer in all innocence. Then—

"Happy art thou who knowest the hour of thy death!" would respond Don Juan Manuel, and at the same time strike his dagger into the heart or throat of his victim, whom he would leave dead and bathed in blood, while he returned home, whence was heard the formidable clang of the heavy door closing, after which all remained in silence and in gloom.

The most dangerous hours were from eleven to twelve at night, and few, even if in quest of the Holy Oil, would venture to pass through that street after eight at night, unless accompanied by two or three guards. However, some there were, who from incredulity, or from dire necessity, did pass through the domains of Don Juan Manuel, and sure it was that that night, knowing exactly the hour, they would fall victims to the sanguinary fury which the demon had inspired in that cavalier. The fact was that the murders were committed with frequency, that the bodies were found next day with all their apparel and valuables, and that, in whispers and murmurs, Don Juan Manuel was pointed out as the author of the crimes; but the visible testimony was all to the contrary. Don Juan Manuel, although sad and gloomy, attended mass, gave alms, and visited as of yore his friend the viceroy. Who would dare accuse a man so wealthy and respected without even proof to offer against him? Thus all the world talked of the matter, but were content with shutting themselves within doors as soon as sounded the call for prayer for lost souls.

There was in the Street of Don Juan Manuel—probably about where Señor Dozal's superb building stands—a house of poor aspect, which was the property of a *beata*—a devotee—of some fifty years old. One of the errors to which youth is victim, when confiding too much in the other sex, had caused Mother Mariana, as she was called, to take the habit of devotee. Promising, further, to recite daily *credos* of the Precious Blood, equal in number to that of the current day of the month; on the 25th, for instance, she spent a long time in repeating the twenty-five *credos* which fell to her lot. Thus, she never slept earlier than midnight. In that unpaved street, dark, silent, and entirely deserted after eight o'clock at night, there was seen but one light, like a lonely, distant star in a cloudy sky; it was the light that came from the narrow shutters of the *beata* Mariana, who lighted a little lamp before an image of Jesus Christ, that was tied to a post, and she did not close her shutter until after she had said her *credos*. Nearly every night she heard a door close noisily, and that sound occurring always at the same hour caused her to watch until she was satisfied that it was the door of the house of

Don Juan Manuel.

One night, toward the end of the month, when the prayers were long, while on her knees before the image, she heard a moan; she put out the light, and, approaching the shutters on tiptoe, cautiously put forth her head. A man was running, and another, following, overtook him almost at Mariana's very door, and gave him four or five stabs. The man groaned piteously, and fell a short distance away. The murderer left him, and shortly the *beata* saw and heard that a door softly opened, and a cloaked man went in at it.

This door was in the house of Don Juan Manuel.

Mariana went to her bed full of terror, and the following day, when the body had been found, she went to relate to her confessor what had happened, and told him her strong suspicions. The priest obtained an audience with the viceroy, and told him the occurrence, but the viceroy only laughed and told the father that all this was vulgar gossip, which should not be repeated or noticed.

Mariana, however, had told the other *beatas*, and thenceforth the terror increased and the apparitions were more dreadful. It was said that from the scaffolds and rubbish where the cathedral was building, came forth every Friday night a procession of monk-like figures, wearing sackcloth robes and black Capuchin hoods that covered their faces. These faces were decaying and part fleshless, for these were no less than the victims of Don Juan Manuel, arisen from their graves. Those corpses' clothes in the habits of friars marched to the cathedral graveyard with thick tapers in their hands, and chanting, in tones that seemed to issue from the tomb, the prayer for the dead. They carried an empty coffin, and, bearing it to the street of Don Juan Manuel, they brought it back thence, holding a man, bound hand and foot. There was a gallows in the atrium of the cathedral, and they put within it the neck of the man, extinguished the tapers, and chanted the "Miserere." Every week this was repeated, and they who chanced to see that awful procession returned home sickening of fever, and within a few days died.—*Manuel Payno*.

***

It was many years before the partial truth was known of what appeared to be only a tale. Then Don José, Gómez de la Cortina published a work entitle "La Calle de Don Juan Manuel," from which the following brief statement is condensed:

"Don Juan Manuel de Solórzano was a renowned Spanish gentleman, a native of Burgos, who came to America in the Suite of the Viceroy of Don Diego Fernandez de Córdoba, Marquis de Guadalcazar. Don Juan Manuel was on most friendly terms with the viceroy of his day, and he was sent on diverse missions to Spain. About 1636 he married Doña Mariana Laguna, only child and heiress of a rich miner of

Zacatecas. After receipt in Mexico of the uprising of Catalonia, the viceroy became the victim of the Audiencia, which body long had sought to depose him, and Don Juan Manuel was involved in the disaster and reduced to prison by order of the Alcalde, Don Francisco Vélez de Pereira. Don Juan Manuel took his reverses calmly, and was patiently awaiting in prison a change of fortune, when he was advised that the Alcalde visited his wife oftener than was required by mere politeness. Through the influence of a rich and powerful friend, a fellow-prisoner, Don Juan Manuel was afforded facilities for leaving the prison secretly at night to investigate the truth of these reports and the behavior of his wife. Several nights Don Juan Manuel availed himself of the privilege, and on one of them killed the Alcalde, almost in the very arms of his faithless wife. The Audiencia dared not declare the murder of their chief, owing to the cause which lent to it, as it appears that the Alcalde made the wife's frailty the price of liberty for Don Juan Manuel. Thus the viceroy redoubled his efforts to save Don Juan Manuel, and they were confident of success, when suddenly, one morning in October, 1641, his body was discovered hanging in the public gallows—testimony to the dark and mysterious policy of the times. The street where Don Juan Manuel lived, where he had built nearly all the houses, and where he slew the Alcalde was then known as Calle Nueva, or New Street. Now it bears his name."

The first part of this paper is by Manuel Payno, a noted Mexican historian. It is from "El Libro Rojo," compiled by General Riva Palacio, now Minister to Spain, a book full of the historical, bloody deeds of the Inquisition in Mexico.

September, 1886.   Y. H. Addis.

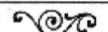

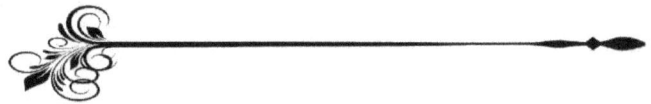

A Fine Haul of Fish

An Aragoneses Tale

From then Spanish of Don Pedro de Alarcón,
By
Y. H. Addis
Appeared in *The Argonaut* November 26, 1888

Covered with glory and with wounds in the War of the Succession and without a penny in his purse, as in those days was the case with most warriors and heroes, the noble scion of Mequinenza returned one day to his dismantled castle, to rest from the harsh fatigues of the camp and eat in peace the lentils that came with his title.

Two words let us give to the soldier and other two to his birthplace. Don Jaime Mequinenza, baron of that name who had fought as captain for the interest of Louis the Fourteenth, was at that day a man of five-and-thirty years, tall, handsome, rough, brave and energetic; little lettered, but jovial and gallant to the last degree with women—particularly fond, indeed, of pretty peasants. Add to this that he was an orphan, an only child, a bachelor, and you have the picture of the Aragonese Hidalgo. As to his castle, it was the same as its master, barring in strength. But as to solitariness, pride and poverty, it was not behind him. It *was not*, for it has crumbled to decay generations since. Figure it half-built, half-cut from a solid rock, lapped on one side by the waves of Ebro, and on the other leaning against a mountain that towered skyward.

At the foot of this rock was a dozen cots and hovels, tenanted by the vassals of the baron, or it might rather be said by the husbandmen who tilled the few fields left to his possession. From the hamlet to the castle the road climbed by fourteen or fifteen steep terraces, above which was a moat, with its drawbridge; the moat filled by a canal or wide ditch that tapped the Ebro a league to the northward, and then fell below the fortress, in a noisy torrent back into the swelling river.

Perched on an almost inaccessible flank of the mountain, separated by this channel from the castle, and, like it, hanging above the Ebro, there was another rocky spur, crowned by a cabin and a little garden, which in that spot suggested the hanging gardens of Babylon. A heavy bean of walnut wood spanned the foaming current between the castle and the cabin, connecting these, as the drawbridge afforded communications between the castle and the hamlet.

On the lordly crag, then, dwelt Don Jaime de Mequinenza, and on the feudal rock an ell-fisherman who had won a rich revenue from the daring thought of building his hut in that lonely and menacing spot. It had occurred to Damian, for such was the name of the fisherman, to swing from the little bridge two vast nets, through whose meshes swept the torrent, so that the teaming eels that rushed through the cutting, toward the mother waters of the Ebro, were caught here on their course back to their birth-place, and held for the hand of the fisherman, who, although he sold them at a low enough price, yet derived from this slippery source a very respectable income.

Yet for all his labor and enterprise the poor fellow could never save a cuarto. He was not a drinker, for all the cold and wet character of his business; he was not a player—indeed, he knew not the terms of *brisca*, con quien, or *malilla*; his *cigarros* were of the commonest sort, and cost him the merest trifle; and for womankind, he had not so much as a passing glance, save for Carmen.

Save only! But then, *caray, hombre!* That was sufficient exception. For—oh, Carmen, Carmela, Carmelita! Here was enough to squander the revenues of an *alcalde*, a *regidor*, a prince—let alone a fisherman. For Carmen was a beauty—a Spanish blonde, think of that, ye connoisseurs!—who would have tempted Saint Anthony himself, if the grace of God should have been withdrawn from him for a moment. Such a waist! Such a neck! Such ankles! And Carmen knew her own good points—none better!—and women of such merit as hers fall in love with themselves when they have not lovers—or when they have, for the matter—and so Carmen spent the price of all the eels in Ebro on aprons, kerchiefs, ear-rings, ribbons, and *fállala* in general, though there was not a soul to see them but her own dear self. Damian, her husband? Oh, but he counted for nothing, less than nothing! For if husbands in general are ciphers, what was this wretched fisher of ells?— a lout, a clown, a clod. Oh! That is quite apparent; convinced, no doubt, of her high mission in this poor world of sorrows, Carmen every day dressed herself as if she were going to a ball or a *función*, and sat herself down at the door of a cabin, where she was seen of the birds, the rock-thyme, and the skies—and of naught else. Still, she awaited tranquilly the moment of her destiny.

In the days when Carmelita first took up her station at the door thus "dressed with parsley," the castle of Mequinenza was still without Don Jaime, its master, and no human eye beheld her from closer range than that of the sands below, whence she looked like some great blossom set on the edge of the precipice. Her husband had forbidden her to go down to the village in his absence, and she obeyed him implicitly, because it is the will of God that wives obey their husbands, and because—well, because there was nothing pleasing to her in the rustic youths of the village. How should they please her any more than her husband?—they, like him, rough, badly clad, and dirty, with thorny calloused hands, burned by the sun, tanned by wind and rain, and smelling of fist from a rod away? And she so soft, so smooth, so dainty, dressed and perfumed like a Madrileña.

It is true that if the poor fisherman was ill-dressed this was to give finer, better raiment to Carmen; that if the husband should labor less, to the end of sparing his hands, the wife would have worked far harder, with the result of spoiling her white ones; true, also, that those eels, which were indeed ill-smelling, paid for the sweet-scented soaps in which Carmen delighted. But who makes such observations to a woman? Above all, if that woman is nineteen years old and pretty, airy, and graceful as the rainbow with its seven colors. Ah, yes! gratitude may well be a sentiment too sober for a young woman, and justice—fairness—an uncomfortable idea for a joyous imagination. These virtues are born of suffering, and Carmen was almost quite happy.

Given these condition, it was not at all inconsistent that the thoughts and interest of the fisherman's wife should turn to Don Jaime de Mequinenza, from the day that the news of his return to his baronial halls came to the village at the cliff's foot. And in effect, when she set eyes upon his worship, Carmen's butterfly brain and her un-loyal heart alike sung to her that this was a lord, a fine gentleman, and a hero—here was a man worthy of beauty and charm like hers.

As for the lord of the manor he was already in love with her species, and as the greater includes the less, he was undoubtedly smitten with Carmen. It was not long before they told each other, by the telegraphic code of looks and signals. Their mutual and respective sentiments, but this platonic system became to both alike insupportable.

In the meantime Damian went on fishing.

Now, whether it came to pass that the people of the hamlet, failing to realize and appreciate their abject contemptibility, came to criticize the doings of their feudal master, or whether the fisherman chanced to remember that his wife was a pretty woman and Don Jaime a hot-blooded gallant, and that the castle and the cabin were not so widely separated—there came a time when this worthy husband displayed less than his eagerness to make his frequent rounds of his eel-traps. He developed, also, certain rheumatic twinges in his left knee, that impaired his agility in walking, and so he hired a strapping lad whom he made his substitute in conveying the eel-baskets among the purchasers of the vicinity. This procedure of the fisherman was far from meeting with the approval of Carmen and Don Jaime.

One beautiful May evening the two spouses sat at the door of their cabin and watches the sinking sun—the same sun in those days of a century and a half since that we see now above us. That evening it was sinking as slowly and majestically as if it expected never to rise again. It was one of those splendid and solemn moments in which it seems that the world has reached for the first time its apogee of beauty; a melancholy hour in which the soul appears to assist at the tragedy of the day's death as at a new occurrence, which will not be repeated.

Carmen and Damian, regarding that sun, whose rays dyed the horizon with a strange prophetic light, felt their very souls stirred within them. Uncultured and rude of nature as they were, they could but feel that this was a critical hour, full of doom, of mystery, of fatality.

When the sun had set entirely both breathed heavily, as those who have completed a long and severe task. The tacit compact was signed between them, each to his own crime, not to be renounced, but irrevocable, as the death of the day that was expiring. They looked at each other full of unreservedly. Damian lifted his eyes to the castle, on whose topmost terrace stood the Baron of Mequinenza, whom he saluted. The lord has his eyes fixed on Carmen, who also saluted him easily. Damian stretched his rheumatic leg, and turning to his wife, said, dryly: "I think my leg is well again. I feel the pangs no longer. I think I will go down to the village and stay the night there. There is a fellow owes me some money; he will be in with his pay near midnight, and I will catch him before he spends it. I will come up in the morning in time to take out the fish of to-night's fish. *Ea*, Carmelita, God be with thee."

"Good-by, Damian," said Carmela, mechanically.

They had never before parted in this way, but to both it seemed quite natural. Damian took his hat and his staff and crossed the walnut-wood bridge-way and the fosses of the castle. The sun was still gilding the peak of the distant mountain.

Twelve hours later the sun once more shone over the cabin. All the sadness and foreboding of the day before had been pure farce. There was the sun again, red and joyous as ever, climbing up the heavens as blithely as if this was his first journey there, and shedding life and movement wherever his rays reached. This was the sun that, in those hours of absence, had crossed the ocean, had called the noonday in the Americas, had served as a god for the idolators of the Pacific, had lighted the way for mariners in China, had gilded the spices of Hindustan, had kissed the stones of the Holy Sepulcher, and had marked the hour of death for some modern Greeks; and now that sun was returning, full of curiosity to know what had become of two fisher people of

Upper Aragon, whom he had left the night before seated at the door of their hut.

As to Damián, he, like the sun, seemed in better humor than on the preceding evening, if he might be judged by the lively and frolicsome manner with which he ascended the terraces of the castle, followed by some other fishers, all singing the most villainous *jota* that had been produced in their country. They reached the drawbridge, crossed the courts of the castle, still lying in silence, and reached the plane fronting Damián's cabin.

"How loud the cascade roars!" said one of the men.

"But what has become of the bridge?" cried another. "True for you! Look! look! It has slipped from each end! it has sunken into the cutting—it has broken!"

"But how can that be? Such a beam—so long, so well supported by its length! so heavy! and of walnut—a wood as strong as iron!"

"I shall have to buy another," said Damián, shrugging his shoulders; "but come, boys, let the bridge be, and help me with the seines before it grows later." And, taking up the thread of his interrupted song, he began with the others to draw up the eel-nets.

"The devil! how it weighs then!" cried one of his comrades; "thou hast done well with this haul, Damiáncito!"

"At the least it is ten arrobas," said another; "oh, a fine

catch! unheard of!"

"I believe you!" shouted a third; "it is more likely he has caught, not eels, but the bridge of walnut wood!"

Damián only smiled without speaking.

"Do you say that net is heavy?" called one of the men, pulling on the second seine; "well, this one is not behind it. This weighs not less than twelve arrobas—all of three hundred weight."

"Oh! it is a couple of big rocks that have fallen in!" said an envious-minded fellow.

Damián was gloomy, trembling, covered with cold sweat. "So one seine weights heavy as the other," he muttered; "oh! But it can not be!" He stepped up out of the water and slowly took his way to the cabin.

By this time the first seine was coming up to the bank, and in it appeared, truly enough, the bridge of walnut wood. Not all of it, but the half. It was not to be doubted that during the night the bridge had been sawed across the middle. The men who dragged it out were staring with surprise and terror; they started back with horror-stricken faces, shrieking.

At the same moment, Damián appeared in the door of his cabin, with his hair on end, his eyes fixed and starting, and a look of utter stupidity, yet screaming with laughter—a laughter like a voice from Bedlam. He had found his home deserted and the couch of Carmelita untouched by her since the day before. And the fisherman had seen in the net with the walnut timber the pallid face of Don Jaime.

A moment after, their frightened mates drew out the second seine, with the other half of the bridge and the body of Carmelita.

"She, also?" Damián shouted; "oh! I did not look for that, though! I thought she would wait for him in the house! I never dreamed she would run to meet him! But she did, you see! She was impatient to meet her lover, and she went on the bridge to meet him. But I had been there before them. I sawed it! Sawed it! Oh! What a fine haul we have made to-day, boys! A good catch of fish is this we have made boys!" And, shrieking, he ran and shut himself in the cabin.

When the officers of the law came to arrest him they found him still grasping a saw, and the cabin drenched with blood. The eel-fisher had sawed off his left hand, and with the right he still drew his weapon across a gaping wound in his throat, while he gasped, with dying voice: "A grand catch of fish we have made to-day, boys!"—*From the Spanish of Don Pedro de Alarcón, by Y. H. Addis.*

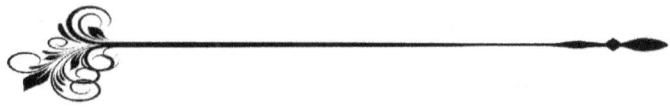

The Priest's Bridge

A Legend of Mexico
By
Yda Addis
Appeared in *The Argonaut* April 18, 1888.

There can be little doubt that the holiest priest, the saintliest man, who ever lived in Mexico, was Juan de Nava. Indeed, it would be hard to fine, in any clime or generation, under whatsoever conditions, a soul or greater purity and self-abnegation, a creature in whom the flesh and its concomitant evils and vanities were more completely subjugated by the domination of a serene and lofty spirit.

Juan de Nava was a man of gentle birth and breeding; his right to the title of Don was absolute and a heritage, not casual nor honorary. He had been reared in affluence, with every advantage of environment and culture existent in his day; and he had some years attained his majority when he embraced the priestly calling. He entered the clergy with calmness, deliberation, and system, as he was wont to apply these traits to every act and situation; and none ever knew what motives impelled him—whether strong religious convictions and irresistible spiritual promptings, or the residual bitterness of some worldly distress or disappointment. The fact remained, Juan de Nava made over all his worldly goods to the guild of his election when he was gowned in Salamanca, and devoted his life to the comforting of souls and the doing of charities. Simple, unassuming, retiring as he was, his fame spread apace, and for one of his numerous deeds of generous heroism he was decorated by the king with the Cross of Calatreva.

It was shortly after this that the whole city was unaffectedly heart-stricken by the news that the beloved priest had solicited, and after much protest and remonstrance, had obtained, from his ecclesiastical superiors, permission to go across the seas to the capital of New Spain. There was inevitably much conjecture as to the object or motive of such a departure. Some maintained that the priest, by nature modest, retiring, and self-depreciative, was shocked and abashed by the publicity and honors that had been laid upon him of late. Others, of the more romantic faction, asserted that he fled to Mexico to escape contact with one who had been chiefly concerned in his renunciation of the world and entrance to the priesthood. Still others, practical souls, expressed their belief that the good father was actuated solely by churchly zeal; and surely this opinion seemed to be justified by the existing conditions. The conquered Mexicans were neglected and abused, body and soul, by their conquerors, who looked upon them as so many chattels for profitable service. Moreover, from the clerical standpoint, an assignment to Mexico was looked upon as about the most undesirable of benefices, indeed, tantamount to an exile—a penalty. So that here, if anywhere in a world of sorrows, was a field of promise for missionary labor.

Juan de Nava crossed the ocean, and was lost to those who had known him, save when from time to time came back reports of his saintly life and zealous ministrations.

In Mexico it soon came to pass that this man was regarded as almost more than human. So holy was his life that all the prelates in Mexico, deans, canons, the *oidores* of Inquisition, all the magnates confessed to him, and what slight curb was put upon their license was the result of his admonition. But with his spiritual ministrations ceased Juan de Nava's relations with the class which comprised his social equals. He lived with and for the poor and lowly, and dwelt among them. As his worldly goods had accrued to the church with his taking of orders, so he bestowed upon his wretched charges whatever reverted to him of fees or tithings, and very often he found himself without a penny toward provision for the morrow; and then this man, who had been the guest of royalty, turned his steps to the dwelling of some citizen, and asked for food like any mendicant, in all simplicity.

It was in great measure this poverty that determined his place of abode. The Spanish conquerors, having razed the Aztec city, filing up the canals with its débris, had marked out for themselves a district, outline by a deep cutting called La Traza, the which was spanned by a few bridges leading to the outlying quarters where dwelt the Indian population, who, for fear of treachery or insurrection, were forbidden to remain within La Traza after certain hours of the evening. The good priest Juan de Nava lived beyond the Traza, among the Indians, who were his chief interest; this partly for the sake of the influence to be maintained by constant association, and partly because of his extreme poverty, which precluded his dwelling within the city. The passage of the bridge was open to him at all hours, and he came and went at midnight fearlessly, as he moved through the most disreputable and dangerous quarters of the city, which had by this time come to have a quite unenviable reputation. The lowest and most vicious of the people bent before him, and ran to kiss his hand as he passed among them, full of reverence for this spirit that shrank not from their most dreadful or revolting features.

And, save the light of his own charities and heroisms, there was no brightness in the life of Juan de Nava, till the day that Beatriz de Millan came to him. He stood in a miry street, admonishing with gentle severity an Indian who had been beating his donkey, when the child approached, a slender, delicate creature, and timidly asked an alms. The priest looked long in her face, as he questioned her. The story she told, if sad enough, was simple. She had lived in a great city, different from this, and less ugly. She had come in a great ship, and her mother had died on the water. Her father had been with her for a time here in Mexico, but one day he had gone away, and she had not been able to find him. Juan de Nava took the child by the hand, and led her to where simple, wholesome food was set before her, and when she had satisfied her bitter hunger, he took her across the Traza, to his own poor home, that should be hers thereafter.

There was somewhat of a change came into his life from this day. He spared himself no more than of old, but he varied his labors. He returned to his home at such hours as were most suitable for the hearing of lessons, and the training he gave to Beatriz was deep and thorough. And the hours of instruction concluded, Juan de Nava again bent his steps back to the teeming streets, overcrowded with a population of the most miserable of God's creatures, among whom he labored often until long past midnight. As may be supposed, as his adopted daughter grew toward womanhood, the good priest could but perceive that he must not leave her at home, alone and unprotected. Therefore, he increased his household by the addition of an aged woman, the mother of one of his confreres, who was but too happy to encounter such a refuge, and lend to Beatriz de Millan the protection of her presence.

The priest's adopted daughter grew up a noble woman. Not a lady of the vice-regal court could compare with her in beauty, yet she was modest and retiring as any mountain violet, as if she had lived in a world apart from the city of feverish loves and hates, ambitions, intrigues, and gallantries. She was more learned than most men, in those days of careless ignorance, yet skilled in all the womanly knowledge. The nuns of a convent, where Juan de Nava was confessor, had taught her the cunning of their broideries and all manner of handiwork; and the simple fare and the ascetic care-taking of Juan de Nava's household was all the work of the maiden.

Withal, she was devout and pious. Her guardian had taught her that, while good works are of greater import than all the forms of observance, somewhat of the daily doing of offices is needful, if but for the sake of example. Therefore, she rose betimes, and went to hear early mass. She had long knelt at the altar of one of the minor churches, near the dwelling of her guardian; but the suburb grew disorderly, and more than once unseemly, drunken brawls had been brewed at the very door of the temple. Therefore, Juan de Nava bade his ward go rather to San Hipólito, somewhat farther within the city.

And there it was that Beatriz was first seen of Domingo Sarraza, "the religious rake," as the viceroy called him, in converse with the *oidor* Amasa. He was of noble birth, this *calaverón*, this young profligate of the first water, and wealthy as he was handsome. He spent his money in torrents, on every caprice, on every extravagance of luxury and ostentation. He was the most gorgeous paraphernalia of the annual festivals of *El Pendón,* and to say this implies, indeed, much. On these occasions, on the thirteenth of August of every year, the day of San Hipólito, *El Pendón*—the standard of Cortez—was carried in triumph, escorted by a great cavalcade of Spaniards, from Palacio Municipal to the church of San Hipólito, in commemoration of the fact that on this date Cortez achieved the final capture of the Aztec city. And to shine preëminent in these processions was the ambition of every young Spaniard in Mexico, and each tried to outvie all others in the sumptuousness of his appointments. But, year after year, notwithstanding the efforts of his competitors, the palm for elegance and costliness fell to the share of Domingo Sarraza.

But not all his lavish expenditure nor his affectations of jovial good-fellowship could make the young man popular. It was not alone that he was a scoundrel of gross vices. That might have been overlooked, for the tastes of the day were not squeamish, and a reputation for gallantries and rakishness was then as now deemed a feather in the cap of a man, rather than otherwise. There was Diego de Fajardo, and Luis del Rió, Antonio Méndez Torres, and a store of others, the idols of the city, notwithstanding—perhaps, indeed, because of—their wild bouts and excesses. But Sarraza was not of them. There was a malignancy in his vices that repelled the others, happy-go-lucky young fellows that they were, and they shrank from his companionship. He got a good many disdainful names, too, from them—"the friar," "the pious one," and divers such pseudonyms, in consequence of his hypocritical zeal in churchly matters. In former days, his blasphemies had been so rank and blatant that it had been threatened that he should expiate them in the *hoguera*, the burning-place of the Inquisition, in front of San Diego, where now run the leafy walks of the pleasant Alameda. Such a menace from the holy office might well intimidate the bravest man in those days, and Domingo Sarraza was no hero. He hastened to feign a serious frame of mind, to pretend conversion and repentance, and to perform all the churchly offices, to avert the realization of the sinister prophecy. By day and by night he wore a cross on his bosom, and as regularly as the day rolled around, he attended mass like any devotee. It was this spurious piety, perhaps, that was most distasteful to those who should have been the associates of

Sarraza, but it was not altogether cowardice that kept him in the path he followed, although this had been the original impelling motive. It was at church that the dames and damsels of Mexico assembled most freely, and in church or on the way thence or thither that they were most easy of access for the utterance of an initiative gallantry or the tendering of a tentative missive. By no means the fewest of Domingo Sarraza's adventures had befallen since he had adopted his new mode of life, and he grew, if such a thing were possible, daily more and more corrupt and evil, in view of the immunity he enjoyed, protected by his cloak of pious seeming.

Thus it was that when he saw Beatriz de Millan first at San Hipólito, his favorite field of prey, he lost not time in following the beautiful girl, in whose garb he recognized the stamp of obscurity and poverty. He was, indeed, somewhat abashed or startled when his quarry entered the abode of Juan de Nava. But his dismay was only momentary, and he found an extra zest in the thought of despoiling and defiling the hearth of the saintliest man in Mexico. From that day, Sarraza lived only for the conquest of Beatriz de Millan. It seemed to him, in the first instance, that the undertaking would be an easy one, in view of the youth of the girl, her extreme beauty, that argued vanity and facile inclination, beside the advanced age of her only protector, and her exposed situation in general.

But he had reasoned in ignorance of the character of the maiden. Good blood and noble coursed in the veins of Beatriz de Millan, and blood will tell, prate how we will of the equality of man. Moreover, she had not grown up under the fostering care of Juan de Nava without absorbing much of the stern and lofty integrity that characterized the man. Domingo Sarraza tried, in turn, each of the specious art by which the social bird of prey seeks to possess himself of his victim, and he found each line of procedure equally ineffective. If Beatriz had raged, protested, shown indignation ever, her persecutor would have found in such demonstration satisfaction, as indicative of possible alteration of sentiment in the future. But no hope or delusion was to be derived from her serene indifference, slightly tinged with repulsion, like her impersonal distaste felt for some loathsome creature, quite apart from her sphere of being. But this was the attitude, above all others, most calculated to sting Sarraza to frenzy, and stir in his heart a score of latent evil passions, that seethed and strained like a knot of inter-coiled, writhing reptiles.

Recognizing in Beatriz the strength of her adopted father's teachings, he grew to include the priest in the rancor he felt against the maiden—a rancor that grew to deadly venomous hatred. But Juan de Nava, when he learned of the young debauchee's persecution, had taken care to surround Beatriz with more adequate safeguards than those of former days, that no foe might come near, to bring upon her unmerited calamity. But if the old man dreamed that he might become the object of Sarraza's vengeance, he took no measures to protect himself from violence, but went and came at all hours, wherever he could give aid, hope, or consolation to suffering humanity.

Thus it happened that he one night neared the bridge across the Traza, as the bells of the city towers sounded midnight, and saw, without apprehension, in the shadow, the indistinct shape of a man who leaned on the parapet. Juan de Nava drew near with the halting steps of age, and the man in the shadow, sinisterly muffled, moved forward to the footpath, seemingly to await the other.

Juan de Nava, accustomed to be hailed at all hours and in all places, in behalf of the dying or the distressed, paused and spoke to the silent figure: "The peace of God be with thee, son. Can I do aught to serve thee?"

"Ay!" Domingo Sarraza answered; "thou canst take thyself and thy prating hypocritic scruples where thou wilt interfere no more with the satisfaction of thy fellows, and the delights of youth and warm blood!" and with that he raised his arm and struck down swiftly, and there was a horrible sound of grating, as there crashed through bone and brain the point of his dagger, driven home so deeply that all the force of Sarraza could not withdraw it.

The old man fell like a log at the feet of his assassin.

Domingo Sarraza made a great effort to detach the dagger, and finding it futile, gathered in his arms the body, so little of weight in its attenuation, and hurled it over the parapet into the canal beneath.

At home, Beatriz de Millan waited for her adopted father, who returned to her never again.

Never had Mexico been so excited and shaken as over the mysterious disappearance of Juan de Nava. There was no system of police, save the body of *serenos*—the night-watchmen—who were a shade worse than nothing, since they never dreamed of interfering in the nefarious transactions of night-birds, whereas their lanterns often served as auxiliaries to evil-doers. But volunteer searchers turned out by hundreds, and scoured every quarter where it was imagined the old man might have fallen alone, a victim of sudden illness. For it was not even remotely imagined that foul play could have touched him, beloved as he was by all, and known to all the city. But the waters of the canal were silent, and the echoes of the bridge, and Domingo Sarraza, too, knew how to keep his guilty secret.

Thus the matter passed among the unfathomable mysteries. Beatriz de Millan, ever mourning over the unknown fate of the missing man, and left quite alone in the world, took the veil at Santa Teresa, though more than one home was open to her, for her own sake and the sake of Juan de Nava.

Years passed. The memory of the priest had become a sort of legend of holiness, and his adopted daughter was forgotten. Domingo Sarraza lived, still kept his youthful semblance, and still continued to enact the anchorite in the churches—and the devil elsewhere. As of old, he was wont to seek new prey before the altar, and in the Sagrario, adjoining the cathedral, he saw, one morning, a woman who awoke in him the instinct of pursuit and conquest more strongly than he had felt it for years past.

He saw not her face, for she was closely veiled; but the charming grace of her movements and the elegance of her figure gave for Domingo Sarraza the assurance of great beauty. He was flattered, too, by the continuity with which she cast upon him stolen glances that burned through the lace of her veil, and the mystery of this behavior heightened the charm of her. He followed her out of the church, across the plaza, through the teeming streets, and before he knew his bearing, he found himself upon the bridge across the Traza, where he had not set foot since the death of Juan de Nava.

The woman paused before him, and let him approach her.

"I dare not linger now," she murmured, "there are people coming, and I am in danger. I will meet you here at midnight. We will be safe when the bridge is deserted." And she glided on like a moving shadow, and was lost to the sight of Sarraza.

The man was filled with misgivings and terrors, but he was also bewitched by the nameless charm of the unknown woman. Thus it was that he found himself impelled, albeit, indeed, against his own volition, to keep tryst upon the bridge at midnight.

The clocks were striking the hour as he reached the spot, for he had dallied, hoping that the lady might be before him; but the bridge was empty. The violence of the passion he had conceived for the mysterious woman held Sarraza spellbound, and he found a score of reasons to excuse her tardiness. Her rich but sober habit, which was almost the garb of mourning, had made him suspect that she might be a widow, whose social position would constrain her to extreme precautions against the discovery of her levity. Again, he fancied her a married woman, and the inconvenient, unsuspected presence of her husband might account for her detention. In short, there was no resource but waiting, for Sarraza was madly impassioned of this last victim of his fascinations.

He leaned on the parapet of the bridge and looked down into the water. The ferns and water-plants on the margin, dimly discernible from the bridge in the ghostly moonlight, lent a more than common gloom to the somber canal and its sluggish, heavy water, that already, at that day, served as a vehicle for the refuse of the quarter. The surface of the water and the depth of the cutting were full of sinister shadows and weird reflections.

As Domingo Sarraza gazed downward, it seemed to him that there arose from under the water a horrible sound, a dull and awful clamor. His soul beat and throbbed in horrified revolt against its bodily habitation, and his body sickened and shivered under the resistance of its tenant. His limbs trembled with faintness, his blood ceased flowing, his eyes were filled to bursting. A cold wind swept over him, he inhaled a sickening odor of dank mould and decay, a grasp as of bands or fingers of steel closed around his pulsing throat, the sky turned black before him, and uttering one great cry, that was answered by an infernal laugh of mockery, Domingo Sarraza reeled and fell on the causeway lifeless.

Some Indian hucksters, wending their way to the city market, stumbled over the body lying there, in the early morning, and fleeing affrighted, gave notice. The patrol was ordered out.

Stark and livid lay the corpse of Sarraza, and across it lay water-soaked bones—the bones of a skeleton, whose fleshless fingers were fastened on the throat of the dead man in a grip so firm that they could not be loosened. From the skull of that grisly horror projected the handle of an old and rusty dagger, firmly imbedded, that bore the name and arms of Domingo Sarraza, and wrapped about its waist was a rosary, whose crucifix was dimly deciphered "Juan de Nava."

The canals are leveled full with the surrounding country, but this spot where two men met with violent deaths is still known as *Puente del Clérigo*—The Priest's Bridge.

Y. H. Addis.   CITY OF MEXICO, April, 1888.

The Palms of Treasure Cove

By
Y. H. Addis
Appeared in *The Argonaut* July 16, 1888.

Of the pacific, and bathes is beauty the sands of a lonely beach, where the waves are braking gently. This is a *barra*—tidal creek, and its 'cove is smooth and peaceful, being well protected by a line of breakers that here lie farther out from the shore than is usual in such places. Black against the backing-ground of crimson and gold with which the great orb decks his descent to his tomb, a boat looms up, rounding the point from the sea into the creek, thence opening inland and presently the frail vessel grounds and two men leap ashore and draw the canoe up beyond danger drifting.

So brief is the twilight of the tropics that it is fairly

nightfall as they alight on the bank. The stars are coming out and reflect themselves in the sea, and far away gleam the lights from scattered cabins. The chattering blackbirds have flown home to their night-haunts, and the belated gulls are winging toward their craggy nests. In the edge of the darkened water the mangroves rustle sadly, the broad banana leaves wave in the plantations farther inland toward the savannahs. The mournful cry of the lurking jackal resounds from the thicket, and from the forest comes the roar of the tiger—the jaguar, while a thousand insects call from the jungle. Nature seems calling to rest; sea, heaven, and earth, all animated creatures appear to be at prayer. The only sounds of activity are the splashes of the countless fish that leap into the air and fall back into the placid, onward-flowing water of the *barra,* and the fitful gleam of the myriad firefly against their formless background. Even these, however, show the light of their greenish, phosphorescent lamps but languidly, as they lacked energy or stimulus for a more sustained glow.

The men from the boat, who had set down upon the bank, as if weary from their task of rowing, arise as the moon climbs slowly up from the horizon, and turn to where their canoe lay canted upon the sands.

"Just yonder in the thicket," says one, "is the spot I have marked out on the parchment that we have left in your sea-chest, that each of us might be able to trace the way again should aught befall the other. You can see the palms I spoke of, two tall but slender ones, growing close together."

"I see," says the other, briefly; "it is not far to carry, and well enough for us, for the load is heavy enough."

"There are not many who would complain of the weight of it," rejoins his companion, "If it were theirs for the carrying. And it is ours, beyond a question. No one can claim it from us, though if our comrades knew of our having it they might determine to take a share by foul or by fair means."

They have come to the boat now and are lifting out the load from it—a massive-looking coffer, under whose weight the two, with their forces combined, still stagger. And so they go un-steadily up the bank and into the jungle, to the foot of the tall young palm-trees, and there, plying the spade and mattock with a right good will, they soon have dug a pit among the nodding ferns and other herbage, rank and clustering, and with many a groan and straining of knotted sinews, they lower into it the heavy, precious coffer.

"And not to bury our treasure," says he who has first spoken, "to cover it over so well that none but ourselves can find it ever."

"Aye, bury it deeply," says the other, "for the heavy-lying earth betrays no secrets."

"I am not so sure of that," returns the former; "as the sea gives up its dead from time to time, so the earth has been known to lay bare ghastly buried horrors—" the sentence is never finished. As the speaker has been stooping to push into the pit the loose-lying earth, his companion, grasping the mattock, has lifted it now and then irresolutely, and at last he lifts it suddenly on high and sends it crashing down upon the skull of the defenseless, unsuspecting man before him. A traitorous, cowardly murder! The victim falls in a huddled shapeless mass; his body is convulsed in one or two long, horrible quivers, and then that form, so lately full of strength and vigor, is inert and still forever.

The assassin stands stock-still for a few moments, gazing upon the work of his hands, upon the ruin he has wrought. Then he turns hastily away from the spot, and even takes a few wild steps toward the creek-side, but suddenly he stops, returns, thrusts the body into the pit above the treasure, pushing it with the mattock, carefully avoiding its touch with his hands. Then hurriedly, frantically, he throws the dirt upon it, until the pit is level with the surrounding plane, ere he turns away again. The freshly moved earth shows plainly its disturbance, a largish mound remains, displaced by the box and the body of the dead man, the ground about is trampled and indented, and even one spot, ominously darker than the rest, where the moonbeams stream through the palm-leaves, shows where the life-blood of the murdered man had poured out, in piteous waste and spoiling.

But the red-handed one no longer notes aught of this. The silence and the solitude of the spot weigh upon him with a potent, dreadful terror, and his only thought and care is to flee from it. Why, the very palms above his head, rustling their leaves at him loudly, are accusing him, he thinks, with intelligible voices. So he dashes madly through the low growth of the jungle, and reaching the boat, leaps in, casts loose the rope, and pushes off in haste from that shore accursed.

But has he left his sin and his awful fear behind him? Not so. Even here, on the bosom of the tranquil water, a thousand witnesses seem to murmur of his crime. The voice of the distant tiger, that roars in the jungle, he fancies might be the wail of his victim. The luminous wake of a phosphorescent fish has terrors for him; he sees in it the gleam of the ghostly moonlight, filtering through the palm-leaves on that pallid countenance yonder. He is rowing on, wildly, blindly, heedless of his course, and instead of rounding the point, he is going straight on, out toward the breakers. He looks up to heaven in desperate hope of solace; alas! But heaven itself derides and threatens, he thinks, for in the flying scuds of cloud he sees but spectres. On, on he hurries, bending to his oars till his frail bark bounds and leaps on the heaving, swelling water, now growing more turbulent with every impulse this warning! Rather he hears in the clamor the outcry of denunciation. He is in the midst of churning, foaming, angry waters. A black rock seems to up-rear itself from the raging waves, and wrest an oar from him. As he bends to snatch at the shattered fragments, the other slips from his hand, and goes spinning away in the moonlight, as if whirling in a weird dance of mockery. His boat crashes on the reef, whose fantastic mantle of spray, flung high in the air, he takes at the supreme moment for another phantom. There is a brief struggle between a stupendous force and an atom—and the man and his sin are buried in the waves forever.

***

Long years have passed. The two men who once landed here are forgotten, the fate of them buried in oblivion, unknown, indeed, of their fellows. But—who shall say how these things come about?—the spot is known as "The Cove of Treasure." No one knows how, or when, or why the name has come to be applied. There is no definite tradition or legend concerning the matter; but through some subtle medium the association of ideas has become a fixed one. And the two palms have long since gotten a name evil reputation. For the story goes that at nightfall a grisly specter comes forth from their shadow and pursues the affrighted wayfarer. In all the country around there is not a human being who will approach these palms when the sun is fairly sinking, and in truth they are shunned at cost of a wide circuit at any hour whatsoever.

Once again—but the hour is now high mid-afternoon of

a brilliant tropical day—once again a little boat comes around the point, and makes for the beach of the *barra*, and once again two men step on the shore. They stand a brief while contemplative, impressed by the absolute repose of the scene. The broad, green leaves of the bananas are scarce astir, all sensitive as they are to the lightest zephyr. Those uncouth forms that salute the eye, unpracticed though it be, with something of dread and horror, are not rough logs, as might be thought at first sight, but swinish alligators, lazily basking in the slime of the creek or in the shade of the cane-brake. The jaguar and the lizard, too, are asleep, but farther within the jungle, where their more sensitive bodies receive less of the intense heat of the hour. The *huaco* sits in the high *ceiba*—for this tall, silk-cotton-tree will be the first point to catch the grateful breath of the land breeze, when that cool, refreshing wind shall blow up sweetly. The cicada sings his grating, strident challenge, but its measure, far from relieving the weight of the day by a hint of activity, only serves to enhance the feeling of breathlessness, as the cicada-call will do, the wide world over. So, too, an added heaviness comes from contemplation of the hawk overhead, moving in lazy circles.

"*Caramba!* but what heat!" says one of the new-comers, in liquid Spanish; "we have found the spot, there is no doubt, but the hour is badly chosen. Does it not seem strange, Felipe, that we should so readily have found the site described in that old parchment, written in my uncle's scrawling hand, and, oddly enough, preserved in the sea-chest of your father, sent home so long ago, after that last luckless voyage, on which the two embarked together, and from which neither returned?"

"Most strange, indeed," says Felipe; "and for my part, I am still inclined to think we have come on a fruitless quest. They were dreamers, most-like, your uncle and my father, and we shall find their treasure-trove to be but rainbow gold."

"It is more likely," says Fortunato, "that they won it by force or violence; and you know that gold that has been baptized in blood shall not be enjoyed by one of the same race as the shedder of that blood. What have you there, Felipe?" His tone changed from simple earnestness to alarm, as his companion suddenly is shaken by a powerful shudder.

"'I do not know," says Felipe; "I felt that strange, mysterious thrill of horror which is said to be caused by the tread of an alien foot upon the ground where one's grave shall be."

"Pah! nonsense!" says practical Fortunato; "how weak of you to remember old women's superstitions! What I fear is that you may be developing *calenturas.* That long row in this beating, blazing sun, the sudden change to the coolness of this dense shadow, and the reek of rank, decaying vegetation—surely these are causes enough to bring on chills and fever in these lowlands. I think there must be marshes hereabouts—I had a whiff just now of sickening, charnel-like air that savors of malaria or *miasm*. Ha! what is that? A man—perhaps a contestant of our claim, Felipe!"

They are nearing the palms, from whose shade emerges the stranger—a strange, fantastic figure, clad in a torn and dusty garb of nautical mode, and antique fashion. He draws near the young men, and they note that he wears about his neck a clumsy old rosary, holding a massive cross, misshapen from oxidation.

"My friend!" it is Fortunato who hails him; "do you live hereabouts?"

The approaching figure returns no answer.

Felipe grips his comrade's arm in a very convulsion of terror. "Do you see," he cries; "he has no face? He has no substance! Oh, God! Fortunato, it is no man! it is a specter!"

Fortunato gazes more intently upon the strange, slowly moving object, and he perceives in truth that he can distinguish no outline of a countenance. Not that the face is either veiled or turned aside—it is simply vague and confused. Then he notes, concentrating the same intensity of observation, that the figure, which glides rather than walks, stirs no leaf nor blossom, though many must be brushed violently in that close-growing jungle. As the Shape passes little gaps of the open, no shadow nor reflection falls on the still waters of the lagoon, and the shy cranes feeding among the reeds, ever alert to take wing at the nearing footfall of a human being, now forage on in undisturbed serenity, while the timid humming-birds still hover fearlessly over the bells of the convolvulus.

Fortunato hears a crash behind him, and he knows by instinct that Felipe has fallen senseless from terror, but he does not turn. The heart of the young man triumphs over natural terrors, in the highest form of courage.

The Mystery makes an imperative gesture, and Fortunato moves forward in prompt compliance. His ghostly guide recedes through the jungle till he reaches the palm-trees; he parts the rank ferns and trailing briers, and the young man sees upon the ground an antique, cumbrous mattock, half covered by decaying fallen leaves, and very rusty. The Specter signals a command, and the young man obeys that fierce and awful gesture, wrenching the tool from its imbedded place among the clinging creepers, and digging furiously, impelled by feverish excitement to a strength abnormal. He is bathed in perspiration, his face is crimson, his breath comes so short and fast that he can scarce continue, yet his energy flags not.

Suddenly his pick strikes through a mass of rotting wood. There is a jingle of metal, and as he wrenches the tool away, he tears off a great flake of the decayed timber, and lays bare a gleaming heap of gold.

He lifts his gaze to his terrible companion, and behold! no more the antique garb and the vague confusion of outlines. Clear, distinct in the broad light of day, it is a *skeleton* that stands erect before him!

Then he knows no more until long hours later, when the sea-breeze fans him back to consciousness, and he revives, slowly and un-remembering at first, raises himself to a sitting posture and looks about him.

Yonder a few steps lies Felipe, cold and rigid, in the distorted position in which he has fallen. The eyeballs are still rolled upward and the lips drawn back, in the contortion of mortal terror, from which they will relax to consciousness never, for Felipe is a dead man.

Fortunato, gathering up the threads of his remembrance, turns back to the pit he has uncovered beneath the palm-trees, and there is still the gleaming yellow mass of gold, with the bones of a human frame lying in ghastly disorder upon it.

CITY OF MEXICO, June, 1888.   Y. H. Addis.

The Devil's Plain's

A Legend of Mexico
By
Yda H. Addis
Appeared in *The Argonaut* July 8, 1889

It was late afternoon when a troop of Mexican soldiers, moving westward, halted at the hacienda San Miguel. The commander of the detachment ordered the halt for the night. Foot-sore and weary, the rough, evil-faced fellows—evil-faced necessarily, since the ranks are recruited from the criminal and convict element—set about the preparation of supper and the discharge of their regular duties.

The officer in command, Colonel Dario Camacho, having received the reports of his subordinate officers, went to the outer gateway of the hacienda, and sat down on one of the masonry benches which flanked it on either side, a number of peons who were sitting on the benches got up making way for him respectfully. He scanned, with some interest, the desolate plain before him, over which he had come with his command that hot, wearisome day. It stretched for leagues, desolate, arid, and flat land, although Colonel Camacho recalled several ugly fissures or ravines in the ground which sunk suddenly from the view, where there had been among his men some difficulty of movement. It was all one uniform gray-brown color, save where, here and there, a yucca stood up in aggressive brittleness, or where a shapeless patch of mongrel green showed the presence of a bunch of prickly-pear cactus. It was not an enlivening or attractive prospect and the good Colonel fell to musing with a certain cynical compassion on the people whom taste or fate had settled in such a spot.

The sun set, and with nightfall the surroundings seemed a bit less harsh and disheartening, for the mantle of darkness is full of charity, and covers many hideous features shown up in all their repulsiveness by sunlight. It was a still greater advance toward toleration when the summons to supper sounded; the great, bare dining-room, with its abundant of homely fare, appeared almost a goal of aspiration, and when the dinner ended, the officer, accompanied by his host, once more repaired to the masonry benches without, he thought, as the incense of their cigarettes perfumed the night air, that he must have been in a most ungrateful mood of misanthropy and ingratitude when he complained about the hacienda.

Don Estaban Alcobilla, the administrator—the manager—of the hacienda, was an intelligence person, yet of little formal schooling. He had seen somewhat of the world before he settled down in the wilderness, and his habit of close and minute observation, coupled with a gift of graphic speech, even greater than is common among his countrymen, made him an interesting companion. Therefore, Colonel Camacho sat contentedly listening to him until the hour was far advanced and all in the hacienda, save the two, were sleeping, even the mozo whose duty it was to close and guard the massive doors of the entrance-arch; for he, too, cuddled down on his *petate*, or rush mat, and slumbered on the hard stones of the zaguán as blissfully as if his couch were of down and roses.

Don Estaban was just concluding a recital of an encounter with Apaches, in which he had participated in Northern Chihuahua, when out on the plain arose a stir which swelled and deepened, until it grew to take the rhythmic sound of hoof beats, which came nearer and nearer, and presently, a large white horse dashed madly along the highway. Colonel Camacho sprang to his feet in dismay, as the animal flew onward with the clatter of his hooves now sounding loudly on the rocky steep of the road dipping down into one of those abrupt ravines, which lay just beyond the hacienda.

"Good heaven!" he cried; "Don Estaban, that horse carried a woman! Did you not see the white flutter of her garments, streaming on the wind as she flew past us? She will be dashed to death in the ravine! Let us follow to see if we can save or serve her!"

But the *hacendado* held back dissentingly. "No, no, señor, this is not unusual. Nothing will happen to the lady. You see that I—I know her!" Colonel Camacho was beginning a protest, when the other touched his arm in warning. "Be careful—hush! A question of your people!"

And, indeed, a number of the soldiers had rushed out, terrified or startled by the unearthly clatter. Their commander spoke to them in reassurance, and they returned to their hard cots.

"You are surprised," said the hacendado; "yet, from a practical standpoint, you should not be. You know that we Mexicans, as a general rule, are not given to putting ourselves out for women. Let a lady ride into the courtyard here by day, and, if she were moderately personable, we would all throng about her, full of offers of assistance, full of praises of

144

her valor, her skill, her beauty, full of protests that we would die for her. Let the same woman be in discomfort or danger, under circumstances like the present, when to go to her rescue would involve some personal peril or inconvenience, how many of us but would shirk the unpleasant duty?"

"It is only too true," averred Colonel Camacho; "we are gallant, but we are not chivalric—and we are selfish. It is with reason that our Mexican women prefer, when it is possible, to marry foreigners—particularly Americans. A Yankee will ignore gallant complements in dealing with a woman; he will often keep his hat on, when he should take it off, in her presence. But whenever her safety, her honor, her happiness, her comfort, even, is involved, though she be a stranger to him, that Yankee, as a rule, would die to serve her and spare her suffering. It is but too true, Don Estaban—as to a true respect and regard for women, there is no man like the American gentleman. But—I do not understand; you who are sensible of this defect in our countrymen—how is it you—"

"That I concur in the faults I deplore, eh?" Don Estaban finished the question; "well, my dear sir, perhaps I am less culpable than you think me. The fact is, it were perfectly useless to follow that mad rider who went dashing past us. No human power could reach her; the horse is not foaled that could come up with the fleeing white steed. I know, for I have tested the matter."

"But—but what?— I do not understand you."

"No, I daresay not," said the hacendado; "I will tell you the legend of this stretch of territory; do you happen to have heard that it is called Los Llanos del Diablo—the Plains of the Devil? No? Such is its name throughout this region. The story runs that this arid tract was once the garden-spot of the section—you know we are in the rich confines of the tierra caliente. All the luxuriant growth of the tropics was here in richest profusion. Wild in the forests grew lemon-trees, whose fruits, in size and flavor, were not inferior to those exported in these days, to find a ready and remunerative sale in foreign markets. The broad leaves of the banana rustled, and the light bending masts of the taro, with their plumy leaves, waved and bent under the light weight of the forest birds which came to perch upon them. In the high mountains, the tall, thick jungle, the trunks of the mahogany, the India rubber-tree, and the liquid amber, crowded thickly one upon another; while in their lofty boughs screamed the guacamayas, and the weird, maniacal laugh of the mariner-bird pulsed upon the air so powerfully as to set pulsating the palm-broad wings of the brilliant butterflies which sailed slowly and majestically amid the thick undergrowths. Streams of crystal water rippled through the ravines that you have seen today so dry and stony, and shoals of fish went darting amid their ripples in the shade of the bending tree-ferns."

"In all this rich and beauteous country, there lived none but the poorest peasants. You know, Señor Colonel, what the Indians are in our coastal lowlands—laid-back, contented, they can barely satisfy their hunger, always more than half-naked in this generous climate, and deaf and blind to the glories of sights and sounds about them. From one day to another, appeared among these simple people two strangers who excited their curiosity to the highest pitch of emotion of which they were capable. So wrought up were these people by the striking appearance and remarkable doings of the newcomers that they would come from leagues around to watch and to listen; and I need give you no stronger guarantee of their interest than to cite this triumph over their indolence."

"About this time, my grandfather—it was from him I heard the story—came down here with a corps of engineers to settle some lands near the river San Luisito. He vowed that he had never conceived, even in a nightmare, of such a goblin-like crew as the Sorcerer—for it was by this name they called the old man—had gathered about him. There were men with wax-white skins, men whose hair was like the petals of the saffron-flowers, and eyes as blue as the forget-me-not flowers. There were others as black as the ropes of India-rubber that the Totonacas bring up from San Carlos, and inky hair that kinked in rings as close as the leaves of "siempre viva" plant after a rainless season. And the garb, and the ways, and the language of all of them, was, in the eyes of the eager watchers, simply monstrous. The engineers had tried to scrape acquaintance with the old fellow in the first days of his appearance, but his treatment of them was so cavalier, not to say brutal that they never again ventured to intrude upon him, and confined their attentions to spying upon him, like the natives, from a safe distance. Ay, mi Colonel, our forefathers were not over-afflicted with delicate scruples!

"Then, there was another and a more justifying reason for their haunting the vicinity—the old man had a lovely daughter. She was a pale, slight creature, but endowed with an expression so seraphic, and a pair of eyes so speaking, that every one of those case-hardened fellows—and we can judge what they were, by analogy, from the engineers of our own days—felt, when once he had seen her, that life was not worth living until his eyes should rest again upon her. But they were seldom gratified by a sight of their divinity. They had lived, the girl and her father, when they had first arrived, in a sort of shack made of sticks, and stems of taro, leaf-and-palm-thatched. But speedily, as if by magic, the jungle was cleared for a large space round about them, and on the disembarrassed ground sprung up houses and their attendant satellites, a trifle rough, it may be in construction, judged by our present standards, but spacious enough. The natives were terrifically impressed by the springing up of those habitations, so infinitely superior to their rude huts; apparently without human activity. For, all day long the attendant crew of the old man lounged in the shade, feasting on the fruits of the region, and chattering in unintelligible language. Several of the surveying party understood English, or French, or German, yet none of them understood a word spoken by this motley gathering, save only in the case of the old man, his lovely daughter, and another, who appeared among them later—one whom they called the Black Man, and of whom I will speak of later. As to the marvelous rapidity with which the houses were constructed, my grandfather always said his idea was that the rapscallion lot did vigorous, lusty night-work, through no amount of night-watching ever resulted in discovering them at their labors. But then they may easily have napped at their post, under the influence of the tropic heat, the five-league ride from the banks of the San Luisito, and the effects of the flasks they brought to protect them from magic influences. The houses were finished, and the old man and his people installed in them; and then came a night when there seemed to be on foot a hellish sort of merry-making—a house-warming, as it were, among a host of devils.

"And all this time, a daily guest of the Sorcerer had been one whom the watchers had tacitly come to call the Black Man—a tall, lusty fellow, wonderfully handsome. Never could they discover from where he came, or in what direction he departed. Watch as they would, he appeared and disappeared suddenly without a word or a token of warning. And, as I before said, among all the villainous gang the only speech which could be understood by my grandfather and his comrades was that of the Black Man, the Sorcerer, and his daughter. And, Señor Colonel, perhaps you will not believe me when I tell you that, among those who knew more than one language, there was not one who could tell whether the words of these people were uttered in French, or English, or their own native Spanish. On the night of assemblage, our friends were present in full force together with a host of Indians from the neighboring ranchos. If you can imagine the scene, mi Colonel! None of them invited, but all gathered there, clandestinely, men of good positions and half-naked Indians, huddled together at the edge of the great, dim forest, full of its remote, mysterious noises, and greedily, eagerly spying—yes; the word is not pretty, but it is adequate—spying upon those who had ignominiously and insolently repulsed their civil attentions. There was luxury in that mansion of unholy origin, such as the simple coast people could not conceive, nor understand; and even the men from the cities found what they saw a little strange and sumptuous. Gorgeous hangings, pictures mirrors, unknown instruments of music—my grandfather, to his dying day never tired of describing the wonders which he saw that night through the windows thrown open to the night-wind, which let them gaze into the brightly lighted salon.

"But—aye! Señor Colonel, the convidados! the invited guests! If you could have but heard my grandfather describe them!   There were creatures, as tall as men, but with wide, flapping wings, like the fox-bat—the murderous vampires which prey upon our horses and our cattle, and that even sometimes suck the life-blood of a vaquero, should one be unwary enough to slumber without wrapping himself closely in his thick serape, and covering his face with his broad-brimmed sombrero. Others there were like monstrous toads and others like serpents, which now wriggled among others, creeping upon their bellies, and again stood up on end upon their tail-parts, finishing with rattles, or whip-like points or other of the caudal decorations of the snake tribes. My grandfather always maintained that they all were devils; and that, by virtue of their fiendish nature, they were able to take the shapes which pleased them. For my own past, I have judged that they had put on garbs of fantastic semblance either from caprice or from some darker motive, for their own disguising. I am told that there are people who find pleasure in thus altering or concealing the semblance God has seen fit to bestow upon them, when they go to great balls in cities. But of this you will know more than I—a poor, ignorant countryman.

"The night had swung overhead for many hours, and yet there was no thought of fatigue among the watchers, so absorbed were they in the strange doings they saw before them. Dancing and leaping and contortions or strange, uncanny nature, such as were, surely, never dear to Christians, and which seemed to the beholders to partake of the character of a rite or service. In view of these things, and of what I have yet to tell you, I have always thought that these people, whom the Sorcerer of the Jungle had gathered about him, were induced to their heathenish faith the Northerners—for such, from the description of their persons, there were—among them. And I have heard, from those who have journeyed and sojourned in those parts, that there is a wondrous fascination, an irresistible spell, in the Black Doctrines of the faith in Voodoo. At last, a burly creature, in the semblance of an a gorilla—but in whom my grandfather thought the Sorcerer's favorite henchman, came forward to the middle of the clearing before the mansion and touched a splinter of *ocota*—a bit of balsam-wood—to what seemed a heap of straw piled up there. It blazed and burned away, and showed beneath a mass of logs and branches, which blazed up so merrily and so far skyward, that they must have been covered with grease or resinous substance, and before long it became a mass of red coals, clear and glowing. Around these, the Sorcerer and his minions gathered, and the Sorcerer seemed preaching to his people—a frantic discourse, punctuated by furious gestures, of which the listeners understood every word in its separate significance, but which, as a whole, seemed meaningless. But his people seemed to understand, for they all leaped and shouted gleefully and frightfully. And now and then were set down before the Sorcerer covered baskets, from which he took, first, owls and serpents, which he threw upon the coals alive and struggling; and the outcries and the bounding movements were louder and more joyous as the hoots of the owls and the hissings of the serpents screamed of their sufferings. And presently he took from the baskets parrots and monkeys; and the human-likeness of the monkeys and the human-like voices of the parrots, as they screamed, sobbed, swore, and entreated, filled all there with horror."

"Then the Sorcerer turned toward his house with an awful gesture, and there came forth two black slave-like women, both stark naked, who led between them the girl, the Sorcerer's daughter. Slowly and resistant she stepped, and in her pallor, and in the dilation of her great eyes, and in her nervous tension and tremor, was plainly to be seen the fear and dismay which were upon her. But the women who were her guides kept fast hold of her, and dragged her close to the spot where the coals were glowing. Then her father laid his heavy hand upon her shoulder; and now every word he spoke was clearly intelligible to the listeners, as was it to the girl.

"My heart has long been grieved," he said, with a look of devilish and sly malice, "over the waywardness of my unruly daughter. Her wicked opposition has impeded us in our work, yet we have always endured her sweetly and nobly." When he paused, a cackling shout of demoniac laughter went up from all his creatures. But the girl stood impassive, her arms crossed over her bosom, with a look of patience and resistance which told she had learned endurance in many a long day of persecution. "To protect us from her evil arts, and to give her at once gentle and firm protection, I have gladly promised her hand to our good friend and patron, who has done her honor to seek it, and who is here with us tonight to receive her and to take part in our pleasures. Come close, good friends, to share in the rites that bless my daughter."

"The Sorcerer threw back the lid of another basket as the Black Man, handsome, diabolical, and smiling with unholy joy, stepped forward to clasp the slender hand of the girl. And then—well, my grandfather always declared that, although he was watching steadily, he could never remember clearly just how it all had happened. The daughter of the Sorcerer slipped one slender had into her bosom and then withdrew it, holding before the eyes of her tormentors a cross which she had braided from the leaves of *palma real* –a the royal palm—which grew thickly all about in the jungle. At the sight of that sacred symbol, every one of that gang of ruffians bent and shuddered, and began to make hideous outcry. As for the Black Man, never went up from a mortal throat such screams of anguish as he uttered, falling like one in a fit upon the ground, where he lay writhing. But the girl's father, rallying from the shock that had at first stunned him also, shouted: "Seize her! Kill her! Or she'll ruin us!" And at that, he and the whole crowd set upon the girl, who leaped across the coals before her, and ran towards the forest.

"Now, not a man among my grandfather's comrades would have gladly sprung to meet and greet her, had she come along or in company less gruesome; but at that moment, in good truth, there were none of them over-anxious to risk their skins for the woman. Moreover, they were arrested by a strange diversion. At the moment when the Sorcerer sprang forward to overtake his daughter, he let fall the creature he held in his hands for sacrifice, and behold! This was neither owl, nor parrot, dog, nor monkey, nor iguana; and as it lay there screaming in the red light of the embers, Maria Antonia, one of the Indian women from the area ran toward it, crying, "My baby! Oh, my Lola! My two-year-old baby! Today at noon I left her swinging in her little hammock, beneath the Marne-trees, her brother was watching her! Why would they want to kill her, to burn her?" And with that the whole mob of her gossips, all of whom had left at home some or all of their children, set after her, screeching. And they threw themselves upon the baskets, set ready there for the ensuing sacrifices, and, sure enough, every *chiquigüite* held an infant. At this sight, even those men stopped who would else have gone to the fleeing girl; as it was, they did not dare, but stood there, stupidly gazing now at her, now toward the squealing, furious Indian mothers. And while they watched, the girl, almost within reach of her pursuers before she could plunge into the jungle, raised again her cross of palm-leaf, waved it, and called upon the name of God. Straightway a noble steed appeared before her; out of the bowels of the earth it seemed to leap, and kneeled before her. She sprung upon its back, and away! Swift and free as light, it bore her!

"At the same moment, the heavens seemed to open, and a storm of fire descended—rain of flame, before whose awful sight, that scorched and blinded their eyeballs, the petrified men who stood there sank down, fainting. It was broad light—at the least, high noon of the next day—when they returned to their senses from that long black out. And then, Señor, believe it or not, as you will, in lieu of the fruitful savannahs and rich forest, this sterile, desolate plain lay stretched before them, dry, stony, and ungrateful, as now you see it. You have traveled today across Los Llanos del Diablo, and you have seen for yourself what sharp contrast from these wastes to the rest of the country, round about them. Even here, on the edge of the forest, we strongly feel its searing influence. So terrified and overwhelmed were they all by what they had witnessed, that they hurried to their camp, grabbed up their instruments and baggage, and, leaving their work in hand, hastened home to Mexico City. The lands still lie unmeasured, as they left them. No one has ever developed interest enough to resume the undertaking. It is only two years since the owner of this hacienda caused it to be established, for the working of a product which, as you know, abundant only in this district, has profitable sale in foreign markets."

"When the company reached Mexico, they found the capital all agog over the strange occurrence. It seemed that, one morning when the Priest unlocked the door of the Cathedral, he found, kneeling before the main altar, a girl, whom none in the city had seen before ever, meanwhile a superb white horse, whom she claimed by signs, was standing in the atrium. The girl spoke Spanish, but she would give no account of herself whatever, except that she had suffered a great deal of persecution for her faith, and that she would enter a convent. When they found that the date of her arrival was that of their terrible adventure on the Devil's Plains, the refugees were eager to see her. But never a glimpse had they until the day she took the vows in the church of Santa Brígida, and then they saw that the new nun was indeed the Sorcerer's daughter. And here, on the site of her sufferings and triumph, she comes unfailingly, nightly, mounted upon her mystic steed, which scours the plains with never-flagging swiftness. In the first days of my stay here, I mounted up and many a night ran after them, on the swiftest horses of the hacienda, which I have always winded, without ever diminishing the distance between us. At first the work-people were fearful, and we could not get them to stay with us. But our chapel has many saintly relics, and our padre is a man most holy, and they have grown accustomed and indifferent to these nightly chases, finding no harm comes from them. No danger even that they will think to speak of the matter to your people, or explain, farther than by a shrug and a laugh, if your soldiers question. But—Señor Colonel! I beg of you a thousand pardons for my imprudence! It is good that you do not have to leave tomorrow, since I have kept you from you bed with foolish babble. Look, over there in the east the day is breaking over Los Llanos del Diablo!"

Y. H. Addis.   CITY OF MEXICO, June, 1889.

The Argonaut Christmas Cover
December 1883

www.ingramcontent.com/pod-product-compliance
Lightning Source LLC
Chambersburg PA
CBHW072356190626
46811CB00019B/918